PRAISE FOR
Mistakes That Made Me a Millionaire

"I wish I had access to Kim's wisdom
when we started Netflix."
—Marc Randolph, Co-founder, Netflix

"All my best successes happened on the heels of a
failure. In this book, Kim teaches you how to bounce
back from any mistake and use it to your advantage."
—Barbara Corcoran, Shark on ABC's
Shark Tank and Founder, Corcoran Group

"Mistakes aren't detours; they're part of
the journey. Kim Perell's book shows you
how to own them with confidence."
—Jay Shetty, Global Bestselling Author and
Award-Winning Podcast Host, *On Purpose*

"A must read for aspiring entrepreneurs—proof that
every misstep can become a million-dollar move."
—Marie Forleo, #1 *New York Times* Bestselling
Author, *Everything Is Figureoutable*

"Most people hide their mistakes. Kim turned
hers into a road map. This book is pure gold."
—Chris Burch, Co-Founder, Tory Burch,
and CEO, Burch Creative Capital

"Building a brand takes resilience, creativity, and a willingness to make mistakes. Kim's book is a must-read for every founder."
—**Sarah Lee, Founder and CEO, Glow Recipe**

"In fashion and business, you have to take risks—and sometimes, you'll get it wrong. Kim's book teaches you how to own your mistakes and turn them into our greatest lessons."
—**Winnie Harlow, Supermodel and Entrepreneur**

"Kim offers real, attainable advice that actually works. She empowers entrepreneurs to move forward— reminding us that even the smallest step is progress. Her brilliance, kindness, and expertise make her truly one of a kind. Every entrepreneur needs this book! Thanks to Kim, I've turned my idea into an empire!"
—**Jill Martin, *TODAY* Show Lifestyle Contributor**

"Think of this book as the ultimate life upgrade— mindset, career, and confidence all in one."
—**Brian Kelly, Founder, The Points Guy**

"Kim's book is a masterclass in turning mistakes into success—every entrepreneur needs to read this!"
—**Bill Shaw, President, *Entrepreneur* magazine**

Mistakes That Made Me a Millionaire

ALSO BY KIM PERELL

JUMP: Dare to Do What Scares You in Business and Life (2021)

The Execution Factor: The One Skill That Drives Success (2018)

Mistakes
That Made Me
a Millionaire

HOW TO TRANSFORM SETBACKS INTO
EXTRAORDINARY SUCCESS

Kim Perell

Matt Holt Books®
An Imprint of BenBella Books, Inc.
Dallas, TX

Matt Holt is an imprint of BenBella Books, Inc.
8080 N. Central Expressway
Suite 1700
Dallas, TX 75206
benbellabooks.com
Send feedback to feedback@benbellabooks.com

BenBella and *Matt Holt* are federally registered trademarks.

Printed in the United States of America
10 9 8 7 6 5 4 3 2 1

Library of Congress Control Number: 2025004890
ISBN 9781637747124 (hardcover)
ISBN 9781637747131 (electronic)

Copyediting by Scott Calamar
Proofreading by Lisa Story and Natalie Roth
Text design and composition by PerfecType, Nashville, TN
Cover design by COVERKITCHEN Co., Ltd.
Printed by Lake Book Manufacturing

Special discounts for bulk sales are available. Please contact bulkorders@benbellabooks.com.

For my four children—John, Elle, Bill, and Jack,
Never be afraid to make mistakes.
The real magic happens in the moments when you dare to try.

Contents

Foreword

The path of entrepreneurship is often romanticized as a straight line to success. We celebrate the wins, lionize the breakthroughs, and put successful founders on pedestals. But what we rarely talk about—and what Kim Perell brilliantly illuminates in *Mistakes That Made Me a Millionaire*—is that the real journey is marked not by triumphs but by mistakes. Countless, necessary, invaluable mistakes.

I should know. In 1998, well before Netflix became the streaming giant everyone knows today, my co-founder Reed Hastings and I were just two entrepreneurs making plenty of mistakes of our own. We spent too much money on inventory and not enough on our web servers (so our site crashed within 15 minutes of launching). We decided to sell DVDs as well as rent them (so we lost money on every order). The first iteration of our DVD-by-mail rental service included due dates and late fees (so no wonder people preferred Blockbuster).

But perhaps our most telling mistake—and the one that ironically may have ultimately saved us—was our ambitious attempt to become the consummate movie portal. We convinced ourselves that Netflix should be everything to everyone who loved movies. We weren't content with just renting DVDs; we wanted to be the complete destination for movie enthusiasts. We added reviews, we sold movie tickets, we had advertising. Our strategy? The classic dot-com mantra: "Make it up in volume!" I remember confidently explaining to investors how we'd figure out the profit part later, once we had enough eyeballs. And had the internet crash of 2000 not forcibly derailed this grandiose vision and forced us to do something that makes money, I'm convinced Netflix wouldn't exist today. Sometimes your biggest mistakes—if you survive them—become your biggest teachers.

And that's what makes Kim's book different. It's not a highlight reel of successes or a theoretical framework for business building. Instead, it's a candid exploration of the potholes, dead ends, and face-plants that every entrepreneur encounters—told by someone who has not only survived them but learned to transform them into stepping stones to success.

As I read through these pages, I found myself nodding along, wincing at familiar scenarios, and occasionally laughing out loud at mistakes that mirrored my own journey. But more importantly, I found myself wishing that I'd had access to this wisdom when I was starting Netflix. How many sleepless nights could I have avoided? How many costly errors could I have sidestepped? While it's true that every entrepreneur must make their own mistakes—it's an essential part of the learning process—there's immense value in learning from someone else's experience.

Kim understands something that took me years to grasp: Making mistakes isn't just okay—it's essential. But as she explains, the real key to success lies in not making the same mistake twice. Throughout these pages, she doesn't just share her missteps; she provides a framework for understanding why they happened and, more importantly, how to avoid them. It's like having a map of land mines drawn by someone who has already crossed the field.

For anyone running a growing company—or even contemplating starting one—this book is indispensable reading. Kim's experiences provide a master class in how to fail forward, how to maintain resilience in the face of setbacks, and how to turn apparent disasters into opportunities for growth.

I've had the privilege of knowing Kim for many years, watching her transform from a driven young entrepreneur into one of the most respected voices in the startup ecosystem. During our time together as investors on *Entrepreneur* magazine's *Elevator Pitch* TV show, I've seen firsthand how she connects with founders, not just through her business acumen but also through a remarkable ability to share her own missteps with disarming honesty.

So, I have to admit that my endorsement of this book comes with one small personal regret. As her fellow investor, I've already seen how founders gravitate toward her wisdom and experience. Now, with the publication of this book, she's making it even more likely that promising entrepreneurs will choose to take her money rather than mine!

What Kim has created here is more than just a business book— it's a companion for the entrepreneurial journey. It's a reminder that behind every successful venture is a string of mistakes, lessons learned, and wisdom earned the hard way. By sharing her story with such transparency and insight, Kim has created a resource that will help countless entrepreneurs navigate their own paths with more confidence and clarity.

But most importantly, the book you hold in your hands is more than a guide to avoiding mistakes; it's a permission slip to make them, learn from them, and use them as fuel for your success. In my decades as an entrepreneur and investor, I've rarely encountered a resource that so perfectly balances practical wisdom with inspirational insight. Kim has managed to turn her stumbles into our confident steps forward, and, for that, every aspiring and current entrepreneur should be grateful.

So, turn the page and let Kim show you how to turn your mistakes into the greatest assets in your entrepreneurial arsenal. Your future millionaire self will thank you.

Now, if you'll excuse me, I need to go prepare for our next season of *Elevator Pitch*—and figure out how to compete with an author who has just made herself an even more compelling investor!

Marc Randolph
Co-founder, Netflix

INTRODUCTION

The Truth No One Tells You

The chairman slid the offer letter to buy my company across the mahogany table: "$235 million." It was the kind of deal entrepreneurs spend their entire lives chasing. This was Silicon Valley's equivalent of a royal flush, the kind of number that would make headlines in every tech publication from San Francisco to Singapore. But I was the only person in the room who knew this success wasn't a result of flawless strategy or great execution. It was built on mistakes—countless, humbling, painful mistakes.

After two decades of building and selling companies, investing in more than 100 startups, managing thousands of employees, and making every mistake imaginable, I've discovered something counterintuitive: The biggest mistake you can make is letting your mistakes break you—instead of make you.

I've made every mistake you can imagine: I've overpromised, underdelivered, miscalculated, overtrusted, held on too long, and let go too soon. I've made mistakes that cost me five dollars and mistakes that cost me $5 million. I've hired the wrong people, ignored my gut, doubted myself, spent too much, saved too little, hesitated when I should have acted, and acted when I should have waited. I've made mistakes that destroyed partnerships and mistakes that built

1

fortunes. But here's what I've learned: Mistakes don't stop you from succeeding—it's failing to move forward after making them that does.

From a young age, we're taught to avoid mistakes at all costs. Success is rewarded, failure is penalized, and doing things perfectly becomes the goal. By the time we've reached adulthood, these learned behaviors hold us back in ways we often don't even realize. We hesitate to take risks, we stick to what's considered "safe," and we shelve our dreams—all because we're afraid of getting it wrong. The result? Unrealized potential, abandoned projects, and a culture that champions perfection while concealing the messy middle where real growth happens.

Mistakes are seen as taboo. In boardrooms, I've watched executives tiptoe around admitting fault, afraid of how it might damage their reputation. In classrooms, a perfect score is still held up as the ultimate goal, with little room for the constructive process of learning from errors. Even among friends, I've seen them carefully avoid sharing their mistakes, worried they'll be judged or misunderstood.

But what if we've been looking at mistakes the wrong way? What if, instead of something to fear, mistakes are the very foundation of success? What if avoiding them is actually holding us back from our greatest success?

Most business books tell you how to avoid mistakes. This *isn't* that kind of book.

This book reveals the untold truth: Success is built in the messy middle between your worst moments and your best decisions. It's about what happens behind the scenes, when you're faced with impossible choices, and everything you thought you knew gets turned upside down.

My journey to making millions was far from easy. I've sat at my kitchen table at 3 AM, head in hands, wondering if becoming an entrepreneur was the biggest mistake of my life. I've watched my bank account dwindle to nearly nothing. I've had to lay off employees I considered family. I've hit lows I never thought I'd recover from. But those rock-bottom moments weren't dead ends—they were the foundation for every million I'd eventually make.

I wrote this book to be a raw, unfiltered playbook—not theory, not fluff, but battle-tested strategies from someone who's built her career upon a mountain of mistakes. In these pages, you'll learn how to turn rock bottom into rocket fuel, when to trust your gut (and when to ignore it), how to protect your energy from toxic relationships, and how to assemble a championship team.

Each story, drawn from a different stage of my life, explores a distinct mistake I made—a mistake that shaped me, humbled me, and taught me an invaluable lesson. It also highlights mistakes I've seen others make, too. Every chapter wraps up with key takeaways and a reflection designed to help you navigate your own journey with confidence and clarity. Ten chapters. Ten mistakes. Ten lessons.

Think of this book as a lighthouse, guiding you through the obstacles and hidden dangers that could threaten your success. Many of these challenges—fear, doubt, stress, and self-imposed limits—are the biggest hurdles to overcome. Often, we simply need to get out of our own way.

Mistakes That Made Me a Millionaire is for anyone with a dream who is ready to break free and forge their own path. My hope is that in these shared experiences, you'll find the inspiration, courage, and insight to navigate your own journey. Maybe you're a recent graduate with a plan to launch your first startup, or working at a company and ready for a more fulfilling career. Maybe you're a stay-at-home parent looking to turn your passion into a thriving business or an entrepreneur facing setbacks on the path to scaling your business. Whether you're taking your first steps, navigating a career change, or pursuing the dream of making your first million, I wrote this book for you.

The difference between those who make millions and those who don't isn't about avoiding mistakes. It's about making the right ones, learning from them, and using them to build something bigger than you ever imagined possible.

Every mistake I've made—and every lesson I've learned—is your shortcut to success.

Are you ready to turn your mistakes into millions?

Kim

MISTAKE #1

Waiting to Be
100% Ready

*That voice in your head saying "not yet"—the one telling you
to wait until you're more prepared, more experienced, more
ready? It's lying to you. I learned this mistake the hard way:
Waiting to feel 100% ready doesn't protect you, it paralyzes you.*

It was the summer of 2000. I was cruising through the sunny streets
of Los Angeles in my black Mitsubishi convertible, singing along to
U2's "Beautiful Day" as I headed to my dream job. I had been working
for more than a year at one of the hottest internet startups, Xdrive—
an internet file-storage company that was a precursor to Dropbox—
and its growth had skyrocketed.

With hundreds of employees and more than $100 million in fund-
ing, Xdrive epitomized everything about the internet boom—a time
when billions of investments poured into the industry, companies like
Yahoo went public, startup founders became multimillionaires overnight, and just about every employee had stock options to fuel dreams
of becoming rich. As a recent college grad from Pepperdine University in Malibu, I thought I had won the job lottery.

I loved the energy, excitement, and intensity of the workplace, working with young, smart, driven people. Collectively, we fostered a culture of fun, creativity, and success, and I kept climbing the ladder— from marketing analyst to marketing manager to director of a new sales and marketing division I helped start, selling online advertising. No expense was spared to build Xdrive and its brand, with a head-quarters based in the swanky Water Garden office buildings in Santa Monica, next to sexy entertainment companies like MTV.

On most nights and weekends, you'd find me at the office with my co-workers. It never felt like a sacrifice because there was nowhere else I'd rather have been. I poured every ounce of passion and energy into that role, acquiring 10 million members and generating more than $9 million in advertising revenue along the way. I believed so much in Xdrive's future that I recruited some of my best friends, promising them we'd all become dot-com millionaires.

By the spring of 2001, the mood at work had shifted. First, there were whispers about a company-wide hiring freeze. Then came the sudden halt to travel, quickly followed by a series of constant closed-door meetings between executives. I convinced myself that this was simply a precaution against the market downturn, and that the Silicon Valley internet companies going under were fundamentally different from ours. We had raised plenty of cash, and my division was gener-ating millions in revenue. But if I had been able to see the financial statements, I would have realized that despite my department's strong revenue, it couldn't offset the company's significant losses. Our cus-tomer adoption was extremely low, our operating costs were sky-high, and we were nose-diving toward bankruptcy.

One Tuesday morning, as I was sitting at my desk, my co-worker Steve tapped me on the shoulder. "The boss wants to see you," he said.

My heart pounded as I walked into the office. The moment my boss's eyes met mine, I knew.

"This is a tough conversation, Kim, but we've decided to let you go," he said.

Listening to him fire me was excruciating. And yet the worst part was grappling with what came next.

"There's one more thing I need you to do," he said. "Fire your team. Tell them to clear out their desks. Today will be their last day, too."

I was still in shock myself, and now I had to deliver the same devastating news to my team. Twelve employees—who were also some of my closest friends—were about to face the same gut punch. I met with them one by one, delivering the news in the most compassionate way I could, but it's hard to soften that type of blow. The whole experience was emotionally exhausting.

At the end of what had started as a perfectly normal day, I walked out of the office for the last time, went home, crawled under my covers, and cried. Every time I tried to talk myself out of bed and into action, my mind shut down, paralyzed with fear and doubt.

How did things change so fast? What am I going to do now?

I couldn't find the answer to either question. The more I asked, the more I spun myself into a whirling panic, feeling stuck and unable to move forward. Within a matter of hours, I had lost my job, my income, and my purpose. All I wanted to do was shut out the world.

I drew the shades over the windows and lay curled up under a heap of tangled blankets. When I wasn't crying or staring at the ceiling, I watched reruns of *Seinfeld* or shuffled to my kitchen in my pajamas to get another pint of Ben & Jerry's Chocolate Fudge Brownie ice cream. It was one of the lowest times of my life.

During that period of self-pity, my mind kept fixating on one overwhelming grievance: I'd poured my soul into building someone else's vision, only to watch everything crumble. I kept replaying the same thoughts over and over: *If only I'd seen the financials sooner. If only I'd had more control over spending decisions. If only I'd trusted my instincts.*

And then it struck me. If I wanted full visibility into the numbers, if I wanted ultimate authority over decisions, there was only one answer: It was time to stop building other people's dreams. It was time to build my own.

I had worked in the internet industry long enough to identify opportunities, and maybe, just maybe, I could start my own internet advertising company, acting as a broker between advertisers and content companies with ad space to sell.

In later years, I would come to learn that when something has just ended, it means that it's time for a new chapter to begin; it means opportunity is coming. But two years out of college, I didn't understand this yet. In fact, I was my own worst enemy, drowning in a flood of what-ifs: *What if I fail? What if I end up bankrupt or mired in debt? What if I don't have what it takes?*

Days later, and as I continued to overthink everything, my roommates finally convinced me to leave the house and go to dinner. Time to shed my well-worn flannel pajamas, take a shower, and at least make myself look presentable. There I was, sitting at a table at California Pizza Kitchen, when my friends asked the dreaded question that could no longer be avoided. "Okay, Kim, enough already. What are you going to do next?"

"I've been thinking about starting my own company," I confessed, hesitantly.

"That sounds like a great idea, *but* . . . are you sure you're ready for that?" my friend Tricia said, her words feeding into my fears. "You don't have any money or experience, and those are pretty crucial to starting a company."

As I left dinner that night, Tricia's words echoed in my head. I didn't feel ready, and it was clear my friends didn't think I was either. Stepping into entrepreneurship felt like walking off a cliff blindfolded.

So I decided the safest decision was to get a job where I could build the skills I needed to succeed. If I wasn't ready now, I'd prepare myself for the future.

For months, I interviewed relentlessly, convinced that finding the right role in marketing, accounting, or operations would give me the experience I needed to one day start my own company. I even started filling out applications to business schools, believing an MBA would help make me ready. I was mastering the art of "productive" procrastination—that deceptive form of waiting in which you convince yourself you're making progress but in reality, you're standing still.

I made the mistake of thinking I was job hunting, but what I was really doing was *hiding* from what I really wanted: to become an entrepreneur.

Looking back, it's almost laughable, the number of roles I pretended to be excited about, the amount of interviews I sat through trying to find the "perfect" job to make me ready. And the longer I stayed in this cycle, the safer it felt. But here's the real mistake, the one that cost me more than just time: I confused busyness with progress.

I was at a major crossroads, and I was running out of time to choose a path. With my savings dwindling and rent due, I couldn't afford to stay stuck any longer. I needed a plan. So, I did what I do best: I started analyzing.

Have you ever tried to calculate how "ready" you are? It's as absurd as it sounds, but that's exactly what I did. Like any good type A personality facing a crisis, I did what comes naturally: I made a spreadsheet and calculated what I called my "readiness score."

I created a "READY" column to list the factors working in my favor, assigning a percentage to represent how prepared I felt. Next, I added a "NOT READY" column to outline the factors that I believed were working against me.

In the **"READY"** column I wrote:

Built a digital advertising division from scratch (20%)
Managed a successful team (10%)
Strong belief there is huge untapped potential in digital advertising (20%)
My passion and grit (15%)
TOTAL: 65% Ready

But the **"NOT READY"** column was brutal:

Only 23 years old (−20%)
Absolutely no idea how to start a company (−42%)
Still get carded when I order a margarita (−5%)
My savings account has . . . zero dollars in it (−30%)
TOTAL: 97% NOT READY

The math made one thing painfully clear: I wasn't ready. If this spreadsheet was any indication, I had no business starting a company—at least not on paper. What I didn't realize was how I was building an argument against my own potential. I had crafted the perfect excuse to stay stuck, using the percentages to rationalize my hesitation and convince myself that taking the leap wasn't an option.

The craziest part? It all seemed perfectly rational at the time. To me, it felt like I was being smart—playing it safe felt like the wisest thing to do. Waiting for certainty felt like being intelligently cautious. However, waiting didn't make me feel more prepared, it made me smaller, more scared, more stuck.

I can't actually pinpoint what shifted but, over the next couple days, my idea came to feel more doable. I started to question my calculation. Maybe it was flawed? What if starting before I was ready was actually the best decision?

At first, I didn't know if this was reckless thinking or my intuition nudging me. But a clear sign was the excitement I felt at the prospect of starting my own company—far more than I ever felt during the interviews I had been having. I started to listen to my gut feeling and tune out the fears of others. And my *intuition and belief in myself* is what I ultimately trusted.

I wasn't 100% ready to start a company, but if I was wrong, I was 100% ready to make this mistake mine.

In everyone else's eyes, this was a huge gamble. They didn't think I was ready, and maybe that was true. But what I realized—and they didn't—was I was ready enough.

Besides, I had nothing to lose. I was already unemployed, and things couldn't get any worse. There was only one tiny issue standing in my way: I was broke.

How was I going to raise money? I had never done it before and had no clue where to start. And with dot-com failures piling up across Silicon Valley, trying to get someone to invest in an unproven industry felt impossible. So, I turned to the one person who always believed in me—my 82-year-old grandma.

I worried that she might doubt the idea, too, but I knew she'd at least hear me out, so I went to visit her and asked if she'd be open to investing $10,000 to fund my internet advertising company. After a lot of nodding, she smiled and said, "What's an internet?"

"A place of possibility," I said.

I described how the internet was going to connect the world and be the place where people would spend most of their time and ultimately transform into a hub of commerce. Nanny may not have understood everything I was saying, but she believed in me, trusted my vision, and wrote me a check for $10,000. A loan I was determined to honor.

I immediately put her money to work with the strategic precision of . . . someone who had absolutely no clue what they were doing.

Step One: Buy the cheapest possible computer at Best Buy.

Step Two: Book a one-way ticket to Oahu, Hawaii.

That's where my college boyfriend John had offered me a summer crash pad. He shared a two-bedroom apartment with his sister and her roommate. It was a tight squeeze but hey, it was rent free and I was trying hard to reserve every dollar of Nanny's investment for business expenses. How was I going to come up with money for rent after the summer? That was a problem for future me.

What nobody tells you about starting a business is that sometimes your first executive office is a corner of someone else's kitchen, where the dial-up internet takes nine minutes—with a full symphony of beeps and screeches—to connect. But I was too excited and grateful to care.

On my second day in Hawaii, I registered my company. That's when I discovered that if anyone thinks the DMV is bad, they've clearly never tried to get a business license in the tropics. After driving across the island to downtown Honolulu, I spent *six hours* in 90-degree heat waiting in line at the business registration center.

The next morning, John gave me a ride to the bank to open a business account and deposit Nanny's check. I was feeling pretty good, until the bank manager strolled over, smiled at *John*, and asked if he wanted to celebrate *his* first business by playing a round of golf. Because obviously, the young woman opening the account wasn't the *real* entrepreneur in the room. John motioned toward me and corrected, "Actually, *she's* the one starting the business." It was one of the first (but definitely not the last) times I'd experience being underestimated. And you know what, I had more important things to do than play golf.

I had my business license. I had a bank account. I had an internet connection. Now, I just needed to prove that Nanny's belief in me—and my belief in myself—wasn't misplaced.

No matter where you start—a corner of a kitchen counter, a desk in your garage, or a dining table covered in yesterday's mail—what matters is that you start. Success isn't about having the perfect setup; it's about taking the first step even when you don't feel ready.

But for every person who takes that first step, there are countless others who don't. They wait. They hesitate. They talk themselves out of it. And over time, that hesitation becomes inaction. I've witnessed this firsthand—in myself and others—what I call the Four *P*'s of Inaction: four silent killers of potential.

The Four *P*'s of Inaction

Maybe the idea of starting out on your own is terrifying. Or maybe you're caught in the trap of overthinking to the point that you believe everything has to be planned out before taking the first step. If either of these scenarios resonates, you're in good company. Countless people know the feeling—whether it's the uncertainty of launching a business, debating a career change, or taking that first step to pursue a passion.

Inaction can shape our path just as much as making quick decisions can, and it often arises from various underlying factors, including the fear of making mistakes, the comfort of staying in familiar territory, uncertainty about the unknown, and becoming overwhelmed by negative external opinions. Let's break down the Four *P*'s of Inaction.

The First P: *Perfectionism*

The little voice of perfectionism first showed up when I was setting up my new company at John's kitchen table in Hawaii. Before reaching out to potential clients and partners, I needed the *perfect* company name backed up by the *perfect* website. I fixated on the name, obsessing for hours, then days, brainstorming, researching, and filling notebooks with crossed-out ideas. I drove John—and, quite frankly, myself—crazy, asking aloud, day after day, "How about this one?"

Torn-out pages and scribbled notes littered a kitchen table already overflowing with printer paper and Diet Coke cans. The pursuit of perfection became a self-made barrier. I had tunnel vision, unable to see anything but flaws, hindered by "the need to get it perfect!" Clearly, the shame of being fired from my previous job still lingered in the background. I had so much pride riding on this venture; it was a pride invested in wanting to prove to myself (and everyone else) that I could do this.

Consequently, the more time I wasted making everything perfect, the longer it took to launch the company. Hyperfocusing on small details had become my Achilles' heel. With Nanny's loan rapidly dwindling, I had to move ahead and accept that the company name and website wouldn't be perfect. I launched initially under the name "All About Special Offers"—admittedly not my finest creative moment. But it served as a starting point, and, within a year, I rebranded to "Frontline Direct." And guess what—no one remembered the original name.

Perfectionism is a peculiar kind of beast that holds back anyone who believes every detail must be *just right* before moving forward. Every step mapped out. Every pitfall anticipated. Every bend in the road mentally navigated. And then, nine times out of ten, life intervenes and reality has a way of unraveling our perfect plans.

There is a difference between having high standards and being prepared, and having unrealistic standards and trying to be perfect. The former is a mindset that's flexible and agile, open to all possibilities within the pursuit of excellence; the latter is a mindset that's rigid and needs to feel in control, within the pursuit of flawlessness.

Ironically, striving for perfection makes you *less likely* to accomplish your goals. Many studies have examined perfectionism, and the common denominator is that "perfectionism isn't a behavior; it's a way of thinking about yourself."[1]

Author Brené Brown summed it up this way in her book *The Gifts of Imperfection*: "Perfectionism is the belief that if we live perfect, look perfect, and act perfect, we can minimize or avoid the pain of blame, judgment, and shame. It's a shield. It's a twenty-ton shield that we lug around thinking it will protect us when, in fact, it's the thing that's really preventing us from flight."

It's a fallacy to think you can ever be 100% ready for anything new. There are so many unknowns that do not become "knowable" until you experience them. If mistakes happen, or plans go awry, you simply learn and grow. The process of trial and error shapes every successful person. There is no perfect time to start. The important thing is to get to "good enough" and then go!

One evening, while John was watching the news in the next room, I overheard a segment in which a Marine general was interviewed about how to make fast decisions in tough, changing conditions. My interest piqued, I peeled myself away from my laptop to go watch it. The general talked about how the Marine Corps created a framework for young officers called the 70% Solution—a strategy that stresses the importance of taking action with incomplete information. In short, if you have 70% of what you need to succeed, take action. If you have 70% of the information you need, make a decision. If 70% of the necessary resources are in place, execute the plan.

In the field of combat, indecision can be deadly. In everyday life, the stakes may not be as high, but the same principle applies: Decisive action can provide the momentum you need, especially if you're stuck, waiting to feel 100% ready.

After watching that news segment, the 70% solution became my mantra. I'd launch new service offerings when they were 70% ready—and let customer feedback shape the rest. For marketing campaigns, rather than overanalyzing, I'd launch at 70% and fine-tune based on real-time engagement. When building my website, I'd go live at 70% and refine the messaging as I went. Adopting this mindset enabled me to embrace imperfection and find the balance between analysis and action.

Exceptional leaders excel at making decisions *without* 100% of the information. They are biased toward action, they create a plan but do not linger in the planning phase, and they move forward despite uncertainty.

Instead of waiting to be 100% ready, I learned to master the art of making calculated decisions *in the absence of complete information*. I accepted the possibility of making mistakes and, ultimately, that was far more empowering than striving for "perfection" and getting stuck in the quicksand of indecision. And you know what else I learned? Embracing this mindset brought me unexpected freedom. It was liberating to know that starting at 70% was perfectly fine, since I could always work toward 100% later. Taking that first step is what really matters—everything else tends to fall into place after that.

The Second P: Procrastination

I've been known to procrastinate terribly, especially when I'm overwhelmed. It can manifest as putting off replying to a dinner invite, waiting until the last minute to book a flight, postponing my taxes until the day before the due date, or letting the mail pile up before opening it all at once.

We're all guilty of some level of procrastination and, if we're lucky, it won't hurt us. But it can become a problem if we habitually delay things because that can ultimately lead to rushed action which, in turn, leads to mishaps, missed opportunities, and unfulfilled dreams.

Procrastination is a common response of the mind to avoid doing something that we dislike or that we find overwhelming. It's often a coping mechanism when we're faced with a difficult and daunting task or challenge that we don't feel ready to tackle. We divert our attention and choose to channel our energy somewhere else instead. We feel like we are "doing" something while still avoiding the most pressing matter at hand.

For me, procrastination showed up as excuses. I fell into the "when, then" trap. "When my work schedule clears up, *then* I'll start exercising," I used to tell myself. "When my boss realizes how hard I'm working, *then* I will ask for a raise." The problem with procrastination is that the more you indulge it, the stronger the habit becomes. Procrastination is the biggest enemy of productivity. It's why, over the years, I've developed three key strategies to help me take decisive and effective action.

Prioritize tasks

Every evening, identify the most important task that needs to be accomplished the next day. Write it down on a notepad or in your reminders list on your phone. Tackle this task first thing in the morning when your energy and focus are at its peak and before distractions set in. If you're not a morning person, find a time that works best for you—just make sure you prioritize getting it done. Whatever time you do it, the sense of accomplishment is what ultimately breaks the cycle of procrastination.

Eliminate distractions

Distractions are a major obstacle to productivity, so take active steps to eliminate them. For instance, turn off your phone's ringer or silence notifications for a set period (I do this in two-hour increments) so that text messages or social media can't bring interruptions. Our devices have trained our mind to be easily distracted, but we can retrain ourselves to be more focused. Sometimes, I retreat to a quiet room or block off specific times in my calendar dedicated to focused work. I let everyone in my house or office know when I'm in do-not-disturb mode, and this helps to create an environment conducive to concentration and efficiency.

Break the task into smaller parts

The scale of a task can be daunting. Breaking it down into smaller, more manageable steps allows you to make progress without feeling overwhelmed by the bigger picture. When writing my first book, I found the sheer volume of work overwhelming. To manage it, I stopped viewing the project as an entire manuscript that needed to be written; instead, it became a single chapter that needed to be finished every month. This way the book didn't feel bigger than me anymore. Ask yourself: How can I break down the task on my plate? What element can be tackled first, allowing me to make progress?

Embracing these three techniques will not only enhance productivity but also lessen the stress and anxiety that often follow procrastination. By prioritizing tasks, eliminating distractions, and dividing large projects into smaller parts that are easier to tackle, you can give yourself the tools to overcome the procrastination habit.

The Third P: Paralysis

Planning your goals and dreams can feel exciting—until it starts to feel overwhelming. One minute you're mapping out your goals, the next you're paralyzed, suddenly questioning if doing "nothing" is really the best option. I know this paralysis intimately. That crushing weight, when a life-changing decision looms, turns even the smallest first step into a mountain climb.

Often, a goal or task can feel overwhelming, leaving you unsure of where to begin or how to reach the finish line. You have a vision and understand what needs to be done, but the sheer size of the challenge—whether it's the effort required or the disruption it might bring—can leave you feeling stuck. And if it's not a sense of overwhelm causing paralysis, it's a sense of fear.

Give fear enough fuel and it can lead to paralysis. You become so afraid that a particular fear will come true—fear of ridicule, of financial implications, of making the wrong decision, of judgment—that you feel unable to take any action at all. But many people don't stop to consider that fears are not facts. We can worry about something, rationalize it, even build a story around it, but science has proven that most of our fears never come true.

In one study, researchers at Penn State University asked people with an anxiety disorder to log every fear they had over a 10-day period. Over the next 30 days, they recorded whether any of the fears materialized. An incredible 91% of the fears were never realized. What's more, one-third of the remaining things they worried about turned out better than they imagined.[2]

One of the first times I was paralyzed in the face of a big decision was right after John and I got married and were considering buying our first home. We were still living at his apartment in Hawaii when a property we loved—surrounded by palm trees and right on the water's edge—came on the market in a beautiful development in Honolulu. I pictured us sitting on the deck in the mornings and watching the boats go by at sunset. But then the doubts started to kick in. *Was I ready to be a homeowner? The company had started to do well, but what if there was a downturn? Could I shoulder the mortgage and expenses if everything went south?*

Days later, the realtor called to say another buyer had made a competing offer. I had to make a decision or lose the house. I called my dad, and he cut through all the emotion with one simple question: "What's the biggest potential downside if you buy the house? If you can't afford to pay the mortgage at some point, you'll just have to sell the house or give it back to the bank."

My dad's pragmatic approach brought clarity. With only a few hours to spare, I submitted an offer, we secured the house, and we lived in that beautiful home for years. By the time we sold, its value had doubled.

His advice showed me how to streamline decision-making by identifying the biggest possible downside and determining whether I could handle it. The next time you feel paralyzed by a decision that needs to be made, it might be worth asking yourself these three questions:

1. What advice would I give a friend in this situation? Considering the guidance you'd give someone else can provide a more objective point of view and help clarify your thoughts.

2. What's the best possible outcome if I take action? Shift your focus to the opportunity and what success will look like. Focusing on the best possible outcomes helps build confidence and makes it easier to take the first step.

3. What would I regret more—doing it and failing or not doing it at all? Potential regret can be a strong motivator. Considering

what you'd regret more can help you focus on taking action, even if it feels uncomfortable.

Sometimes, we delay starting new things because *too much* is in front of us—too many options, too many opinions, too much information. This can lead to analysis paralysis.

We make countless decisions a day, whether it is what to wear, what to say, how to say it, what to eat, where to invest our money, who to hire . . . the list goes on and on! Never before have we had so many options. Where our ancestors may have had few choices about how to earn a living or where to live, we live in a digital and tech age of endless opportunity. Having options is a good thing, but there is also a paralyzing effect that comes with "choice overload," and researchers have found that the more complex a situation, and the more uncertainty there is, the more overwhelmed we can feel.[3] Having a Plan A and Plan B is smart. Having a Plan A, B, C, D, and E can send you into a spin.

Too much information actually inhibits our ability to make decisions.[4]

I've seen so many people give up on incredible ideas and carefully crafted plans—not because they weren't capable but because they got stuck in paralysis. Stuck overthinking, feeling overwhelmed, or letting fear take over.

My good friend Heather has an amazing concept for a podcast but hasn't taken the first step to launch it. She's overwhelmed by questions like "What if it's not good enough?" and "Where do I even start?" Another friend, Mary, dreamed up a brilliant idea for a children's book but spent so much time imagining all the ways it could go wrong that she never wrote it. Both Heather and Mary overanalyzed every possibility until they talked themselves out of action entirely. They stopped themselves before they ever had the chance to begin.

Instead of getting stuck overthinking every detail, focus on what excites you.

You won't conquer the world overnight, and you can't anticipate every conceivable challenge. Even the best-laid plans can go off track, but what part of your vision energizes you? What possible outcome fills you with hope? What about the opportunity makes you feel inspired? When you focus on the excitement and possibility rather than the obstacles, you'll be amazed how quickly you break free from the paralysis and start moving forward.

When looking to start my first business, I was riddled with fear and overwhelmed with anxiety. It is hard to let go of what's familiar and safe. Yet the idea of going it alone excited me—and that was a crucial piece of information. Once I believed more in my vision and myself than in my fears, I had the courage to break out of paralysis and move forward. If your idea scares you and energizes you in equal measure, I suggest you take action.

The Fourth P: Pessimism

The way we view our lives can significantly shape the level of success we achieve. Attitude and outlook are everything. When it comes to decision-making, pessimism is poison.

There are numerous reasons for pessimism—events that occurred in childhood, negative role models, hard-luck stories—and it can be damaging. Pessimism filters life through a negative lens that warps and distorts dreams, telling us what isn't possible. This mindset misleads us into thinking we're not good enough, or we're not smart enough, or that nothing we do ever works out.

Pessimism is an innate part of human nature. Science has shown that our brains are hardwired for negative thinking—a phenomenon called "the negativity bias." Because of this, we subconsciously give more weight to negative information than positive. Here are a few examples of how the negativity bias can show up:

1. You get a performance review filled with praise from the boss, but you fixate on the one critical comment, leaving you doubting your overall competence.

2. You get positive comments of love and encouragement on social media but obsess about one negative comment and allow it to ruin your mood.

3. Your business receives plenty of positive reviews online but one bad review causes you to question your success.

Do any of these situations sound familiar? It's important to remember that not everyone will appreciate you or your work. Sure, it might make you sad, and it's okay to have your ego bruised a little. One outside opinion shouldn't be allowed to define you. So keep things in perspective and don't amplify one comment, one review, or one piece of feedback. The mind naturally gravitates toward critics, cynics, and flaws—that's the negativity bias at work. But, by recognizing this tendency and understanding how the mind operates, you gain the ability to rise above it and take control of your thoughts.

Remember, a thought is nothing more than a thought—fleeting and without significance—until we give it meaning. Thoughts don't define us, nor do they make up our reality. Yet we hold on to negative thoughts and allow them to build into an elaborate, fear-based story. It is far healthier to treat thoughts like clouds in the sky—watch them drift in and watch them drift away. View them as an element of the mind's weather.

I know firsthand how challenging it can be to maintain a positive outlook when faced with negative feedback, setbacks, or failure. I've been rejected, criticized, and laughed at. But I've learned that mistakes and failures don't make me a failure. Success is about believing in yourself even when things don't work out.

Of course, this is easier said than done. Being optimistic can feel impossible when things aren't going well. But I have coached enough leaders, business executives, and entrepreneurs to know that optimism can be nurtured.

A negative thought can arrive almost on autopilot, but you can learn to see that thought, dismiss it, and let it go. You have the power to consciously replace it with a positive mindset, effectively retraining your mind to adopt a new way of thinking.

For example, if you're struggling with a task or project, your first thought might be, *I'll never figure this out. I should give up.* That's the moment when you should counter that thought with a positive belief: *I can do this. I have the ability to figure things out.* Spend up to a minute focusing on that positive thought and even take a moment to visualize yourself successfully completing the task. Over time, the brain's natural ability to adapt and rewire itself—a process known as neuroplasticity[5]—can transform how you think.

Always ask yourself: Is this thought useful or helpful? Or is it negative and fear based? There is a world of difference between a practical thought that serves you and a negative thought that hinders you. You can choose where to focus your attention. With practice, you can lead the direction of your mind, rather than let the mind lead you.

Wherever you happen to be on your journey, the most important thing is that you begin. Take small steps. Keep moving forward.

For those of you who think time has passed you by, just know that it's never too late! Opportunity doesn't have an age limit. Consider the stories of these business leaders:

Vera Wang launched her iconic fashion brand at 40.

Christian Dior launched his fashion house at the age of 42.

Sam Walton opened the first Walmart store at 44.

Bernard Marcus co-founded Home Depot at 49.

Arianna Huffington co-founded *The Huffington Post* at age 55.

Colonel Sanders was 62 when he began actively franchising his Kentucky Fried Chicken restaurants.

My entrepreneurial journey spans decades—from launching my first venture in my 20s to building my ninth company in my 40s.

And then there's my dad, starting a new company by entering the world of carbon-neutral housing. He's 72. Entrepreneurship knows no age!

Success Is Only Possible If You Start

To achieve greatness, you have to take the first step, even if you do not feel 100% ready. Progress and success only come to those who dare to begin. As the great motivational speaker Zig Ziglar said, "You don't have to be great to start, but you have to start to be great."

Looking back on the course of my career and the companies I've started and sold, I know that starting before I felt ready is a consistent theme. In 2021, after 20 years as a tech entrepreneur, I decided to launch two new businesses in completely unfamiliar categories: a clean beauty company called Cay Skin and an adaptogenic tea company named JUNI. You'll learn more about these launches later in the book. Was I ready? Not at all. But I adopted the 70% rule and had the confidence to believe that once I started, I would figure out the rest along the way. Whatever you're starting, learning as you go is key. It's not about knowing everything up front but being willing to adapt, learn, and grow.

I can't stress enough how important it is to take that first step, even when it feels scary. Opening the door to success means accepting that things won't be perfect right away. It's about having the courage to begin without all the answers.

I didn't have all the answers when I moved to Hawaii, but I leaped anyway. Frontline Direct began as a scrappy kitchen-table startup plagued by uncertainty and eventually grew into something far bigger than I ever imagined. At the beginning, my blue-sky dream was simple: Make a million dollars. A million dollars was a number that seemed almost too big to be real.

And then, in 2008, reality exceeded my expectations. I didn't just sell Frontline Direct for a million. I sold it to Adconion Media Group for **$20 million**—shattering every limit I had ever imagined.

I can remember being in Las Vegas at an industry conference the day the wire hit. Still in disbelief, I went to the ATM to check my balance. Instead of showing me the number, the machine printed a slip with "ERROR: *Balance Exceeds Display Limit.*" I stared at it, stunned.

That younger version of me would never have imagined that moment was possible. It wasn't just about the money—it was validation that all the risks, all the sleepless nights, all the times I feared failure had been worth it. Proof that starting, even when I wasn't 100% ready, can lead to life-changing success.

And while I popped champagne in Vegas with my team to celebrate, there was one person I wanted to share this moment with the most. Instead of going home after Vegas, I booked a flight to Naples, Florida . . . to see Nanny. When I showed up at her doorstep unannounced, the stunned look on her face was priceless. "Kim?! What are you doing here? Is everything okay?"

I smiled. "I've got some great news to tell you."

We sat down in her living room, the same small but welcoming place where I had nervously pitched my crazy internet business idea five years earlier. Only this time, I wasn't asking for money. I was there to pay it back—with interest!

I handed Nanny a check without saying a word . . .

"What's . . . this?!" she asked.

"A return on your investment," I said.

She kept looking at the check in her hands, not quite believing it.

I told her how her $10,000 loan had turned into a $20 million sale. How none of it—none of my success, my confidence, my ability to take that first leap—would have been possible without her belief in me. Looking back over my career, no moment has made me prouder than repaying Nanny back many times over.

Before she passed away, I was able to express my gratitude by taking her on some incredible trips, and we created some cherished memories together. One favorite memory is captured in the photo below—the time we went to Italy and drove around in a cherry-red Ferrari. "The high life!" as Nanny put it.

Nanny will forever be the person who believed in me and saw my potential when others hesitated. Without her belief and investment, that dream would have remained just that—a dream.

LESSON IN THE MISTAKE

If I had waited to feel ready,
I'd still be waiting. The mind
builds a cage that limits
your potential. Start before
you're ready.

CHAPTER SUMMARY

Self-reflection: Where in my life am I waiting to start something until I feel 100% ready? What's one small step I can take today to make progress?

Key Takeaways:

- ▶ **Start Before You Are Ready:** Waiting for "perfect" can lead to missed opportunities. Get to a place of "good enough" and go!

- ▶ **Overcome the Four *P*'s of Inaction:** Recognize the forces that lead to inaction: perfectionism, procrastination, paralysis, and pessimism. Overcome these obstacles with awareness and by focusing on taking small steps.

- ▶ **Adopt the 70% Solution:** If you have 70% of the necessary resources or information in place, you have enough to take action.

- ▶ **Embrace Trial and Error:** Every successful person embraces trial and error. Learn as you go. Rather than focus on what scares you, focus on what excites you.

- ▶ **Decisiveness and Speed Are Important:** A fast, good decision is often more impactful than a perfect but delayed one. You can always make course corrections along the way.

- ▶ **Success Comes from Starting:** Take small steps. Keep moving forward. Progress and growth only come to those who dare to begin.

Millionaire Mindset: Every challenge is an opportunity to grow. Each step forward is progress. I'm flexible, agile, and open to all possibilities in the pursuit of excellence. I don't need to be 100% ready to start. I trust myself and have the courage to take the first step.

MISTAKE #2

Trying to Do Everything Alone

People love stories about lone geniuses who build empires in their garages. It's a seductive myth but far from the truth. I made the mistake of believing I had to do everything alone. And it almost cost me everything.

On August 12, 2004, I lost $50,000 on a deal that should have been a major win for my new startup—and it was all my fault.

That was the morning my husband, John, found me slumped at the kitchen table, drenched in sweat, pale as a ghost, face down on the laptop, to the extent the keyboard left its imprint on my cheek. The tears that streamed down my cheeks spoke for me because I couldn't find any words. Sixteen-hour workdays had invited near-delirium, topped off with a temperature of 104 degrees.

Once again, I'd pulled an all-nighter, racing to meet an 8 AM deadline for a client proposal that could bring in the substantial revenue I desperately needed to cover my growing expenses. The proposal had to be finished, so, despite the fatigue pulling at me, I pressed on and pushed through. Until John found me. Until I didn't have an ounce of energy left to give.

As John tucked me into bed, my body shivered in the sweltering climate, and my head pounded relentlessly. This was what the breaking point looked like. Over the previous six months, as my immune system flagged, I had visited the doctor three times for sore throats and sinus infections, and each visit led to the same prescription: rest. And each time, I ignored the doctor's advice and plunged back into work with the same intensity.

The workload had increased rapidly at my new digital marketing startup, Frontline Direct, and I'd found myself working around the clock just to keep up—late nights, early mornings, and fewer and fewer breaks. I pushed myself harder, doing everything myself to get the job done. I pitched potential clients, crafted marketing plans, managed the finances, and even handled customer service issues. I was determined to do whatever it took to make it work.

My passion, energy, and drive were all channeled into a singular focus. Inevitably, the endless tasks and constant pressure to deliver left me exhausted and overwhelmed.

"You can't go on like this," said John. "It's unsustainable."

He pointed out what was obvious to everyone but me. My body demanded change—quietly at first and then with a feverish rage. It demanded more than just rest; it sought something deeper. But that wasn't the most important issue that needed to be addressed. I slowly realized that the real problem was a chronic case of "lone-wolf syndrome"—the conviction that I was more effective, and could achieve better results, by working alone. That was the story in my head. I didn't need anyone else. I didn't need help. I was the architect of my own destiny, capable of doing it alone. That's what founders do, right?

Being found face down on a keyboard can be a sobering moment.

Once the tears had dried up and I'd spent 24 hours in bed, I knew I needed advice from someone who had already navigated the challenges of starting their own company. I set my ego aside and decided to make some calls. But just as I began to dial the first number, I hesitated. In my mind, asking for help meant weakness. The smartest and most logical thing to do—asking for advice—was hindered by a stubborn pride in doing things on my own. I hung up the phone.

John didn't understand. "Why can't you just ask for help?"

I couldn't fully explain it, but when I thought about it, I realized that the roots of this lone-wolf mentality extended all the way back to childhood.

———

Growing up as a twin meant I was constantly in competition with my sister, Tracy. She always seemed to be one step ahead—smarter, faster, stronger. Every challenge, every game, every academic achievement was a race, and she was always in first place.

In seventh grade, we were on the same soccer team, and all our friends and family were stacked on the sidelines for the biggest game of the season. Tracy was the striker and star, earning roars of applause every time she scored. I was the goalie and, whenever the ball was kicked my way, the crowd held their breath.

I vividly remember the moment the game was tied. With the clock ticking, the other team charged toward the net and their striker took a shot. I instinctively lunged to block it, but the ball flew past me, almost in slow motion. The ball smacked the back of the net. I'll never forget the crowd's loud, sympathetic "AWWWWW!"

Seconds later, the buzzer blared. We lost the game.

My teammates were devastated, and I felt the heavy weight of their disappointment. I walked off the field, feeling personally responsible. I'd let everyone down. The crowd. My teammates. My coach. My sister. And myself.

I quit soccer after that season. I didn't want the pressure of being part of a team. Instead, at the age of 12, I turned my focus to solo activities—tennis, swimming, and running. That way, if I failed, the only person I would let down was myself. I became a decent tennis player. I loved that I could walk to the local court and work on making improvements myself. I put in the effort, won a few small tournaments, and those trophies on the bookshelf became proof that hard work paid off. With each win, my confidence grew, and "I can do it on my own!" became my mantra.

It's easy to see how I grew from a solo athlete to a solopreneur. I'm not saying one bad soccer game and a few tennis triumphs as a 12-year-old made me want to become an entrepreneur, but it definitely shaped my belief that I was better off being self-sufficient, operating on my own.

A decade later, that same rigid self-sufficiency was, without a doubt, what led me to near collapse that night in Honolulu. My stubborn resistance to ask for help kept me at the kitchen table, forcing myself to finish that critical proposal—surrounded by medicine bottles, saltine crackers, and half-empty glasses of orange juice.

Days later, having recovered, I received a call and heard the dream words: "We loved your proposal and want to hire you!"

I immediately started planning how to deploy my robust marketing plan. I dived into the project details, breaking down all the expense items and fine-tuning the budgets . . . and that was when I was stopped in my tracks by something I spotted when double- and triple-checking the numbers.

There, on paper, in black and white, was a glaring miscalculation.

My exhaustion had clouded my focus, causing me to overlook substantial costs. As a result, I had structured the deal unprofitably. My stomach dropped as I stared at the bottom line—the account was going to lose $50,000 over the course of the first year, a jaw-dropping amount for a company still in its early days. Within an hour of receiving dream news, a huge win had turned into a significant financial and emotional loss. And I had no one to blame but myself.

If I thought I'd hit the lowest point at my kitchen table a few days earlier, I was wrong. *This* was my worst nightmare. I put my head in my hands in disbelief. *How could I have made such a big mistake? How will I dig out of this financial hole? Can my startup survive this loss?*

As I picked up the phone to call my client, knowing I was about to expose everything I had been trying to hide, my stomach twisted into knots. But there was no way around this. I had to own up to my mistake.

I started by detailing how the miscalculation had happened. "And so it turns out that I underpriced this by fifty thousand dollars," I admitted.

"Excuse me?!" the CEO said.

"I take full responsibility!" I added quickly, "This is on me. Here's how I propose we fix—"

"Fix it?" he interrupted. "This isn't just about fixing a number . . . You've put us in a terrible situation. How do we fix the trust we've lost in you?"

I didn't have an answer. And they didn't wait for one. "This is unacceptable. We can't move forward. Consider this partnership over, Kim."

And just like that, it was done. No negotiation. No second chances.

My ego-fueled mistake had cost me more than money. It had cost me their confidence, their respect, and any future opportunities with them. I didn't just drop the ball—I had shattered it.

But without that moment of crisis, I might never have seen what my pride had buried: I couldn't do it alone. My own stubbornness had landed me in this mess, and I needed to ask for help.

This time, I didn't hesitate. I called Jerry, a family friend and the most successful person I knew growing up. He was a seasoned CEO who had built and sold multiple companies.

"Kim? It's been forever. How are you?" he said.

No one had asked me that in a long time—how was *I* doing? I hadn't even bothered to ask that of myself. Before I knew it, I was telling him everything. It was a full-on, no-holds-barred confessional. And he didn't interrupt me once. He just let me talk.

When I was finally done, he sounded almost amused. "Kim," he said. "I have only one question: Why are you trying to do all of this alone?"

I didn't know how to answer. The silence was deafening.

"Kim, are you still there?"

"Because I thought I had to," I finally said. "I thought it was the only way."

"That is the dumbest thing I have ever heard."

There was another pause as that truth bomb landed, and then we both laughed. For me, that laugh brought a sobering perspective. "I thought it was a sign of weakness to ask for help," I said.

"It's the opposite," said Jerry. "It's a sign of strength."

"So it's a sign of strength that I called you?"

"Absolutely. You'll never scale your company if you try to do everything alone."

It was exactly what I needed to hear. Coming from someone who'd been there and done that—with millions of dollars in the bank to prove it—his words carried weight. No one person had single-handedly scaled a company. His simple advice allowed me to reframe my entire thinking and approach. I now knew what I needed to do. If I had any chance of making it, I was going to have to build a team.

Breaking out of the lone-wolf mindset didn't come naturally at first. After a lifetime of looking only to myself for every answer, I had to unravel old patterns and build new habits. It was a constant practice of reminding myself to think and act differently. And thanks to the wisdom Jerry shared, my mantra switched from "I can do it on my own" to "No one is successful alone."

I prioritized building a team—not just any team but a dream team. One that would complement my strengths and compensate for my weaknesses. One that I needed to make room for at my kitchen table!

You won't be surprised to learn that one of the first hires I made was a head of finance. I made room for Dave alongside me at the table. We had worked together at Xdrive, and he had the best, and sharpest, financial mind of anyone I knew. Plus, he had honesty and integrity and was fun to be around.

Next, I moved the printer to the floor to make room for Steve as head of technology. He was someone I could count on when it came to solving complex problems and automating mundane processes. Finally, I moved the coffee maker beside the stove to make room for Amanda as head of sales. One of my closest college friends, she excelled in building partnerships and driving revenue.

My first team was now in place, and it proved to be a game changer. Suddenly, the weight of the world wasn't on my shoulders. No longer solely responsible for achieving every goal and attending to every critical task, and no longer wearing every hat and juggling very different demands, I could delegate and trust the specialized talents around me that extended my reach and rounded out my own skill sets.

This lone wolf had finally found her pack.

The Four Fears of Asking for Help

In later years, when I really dug into why I was reluctant to ask for help, I realized there were four specific fears that got in my way. I call these the Four Fears of Asking for Help.

1. Fear of judgment
2. Fear of imposing
3. Fear of being vulnerable
4. Fear of rejection

Do any of these resonate? Have you ever stopped yourself from asking for help because of fear or discomfort? Or maybe you didn't ask because you didn't think receiving help was even an option?

Over the years, I've consistently witnessed myself, and others, being held back by these four fears. At some point, we all wrestle with the lone-wolf mentality, whether out of fear, a strong will, or misguided beliefs. It's only when we start to unpack those fears that we can pause, step back, zoom out, and truly examine whether our intentions and approach are aligned with our best interests.

If you can take the time to understand and address the four fears of asking for help, you can disempower the hold they have over you. And once you've disempowered them, you have the opportunity to unlock greater success and fulfillment. With that in mind, let's dive into each fear.

Fear of Judgment

Picture this: You've been asked to give a speech to 100 people, but you've never spoken to a crowd that size before. You don't even know how to connect with that many people. Every bone in your body wants to ask for help, but you are worried that someone will interpret your request as proof that you are not worthy of giving the speech, or, even worse, that you are not capable.

One of the most common fears we all share is the fear of being judged—for how we act, for what we say, for what we share with the world, even for acknowledging what we don't know.

I've been there many times. My fear of judgment was the fear of being perceived as incompetent or weak when asking for help, as if it were an admission of failure. But every person, no matter how skilled they are, has sought help or guidance at some point in their journey. Experience is shaped by the hard work of learning lessons and embracing guidance along the way. Success is built from being brave enough to say, "I don't know how to do this . . . can you please show me how?"

My experience has shown me that the right people won't judge you. In most cases, they will respect you for wanting to ensure that you deliver the best possible outcome. As Jerry said, asking for help is a sign of strength. I would go further and say it is also a commitment to excellence.

Our fear of judgment can usually be traced back to childhood— and it can take root in our lives as early as four or five years old.[6] I still remember the sting of my third-grade teacher shaming me in front of the class when I raised my hand to ask about the difference between metaphors and similes. "Weren't you listening during the lesson? We've gone over this a dozen times, Kim!" she said, marching down the aisle to my desk. I was so embarrassed. It was another early experience that shaped my reluctance to seek help.

We might dismiss these small moments from childhood as insignificant, but they often mark the beginning of our fears—planted by the words of parents, teachers, or peers. This is why the fear of judgment isn't something we can easily outgrow.

I recently conducted a poll to uncover the most common barriers to success. I asked 1,000 adults in the United States which barriers they thought were holding them back from being more successful. The number one response was, "I don't like asking for help because I'm afraid people will judge me for asking."

It's a powerful fear, too. But remember that every time you're scared of being judged, there's a good chance you will be respected for seeking help. Of course, *how* you ask for help is important, too, but as long as you do it thoughtfully and authentically, people will admire your courage as well as your capacity to learn. So don't let fear of judgment hold you back. Simply recognize that it's a fear from the past that has no business affecting your future. Rise above it. Be bold. Ask for help! I'm confident you'll be amazed by the outcome.

Fear of Imposing

How many times has someone offered their support and you've declined, saying you had it covered, but, secretly, you would have loved to accept?

We can all relate to the fear of imposing on others, but science tells us that people consistently *underestimate* the willingness of others to help and *overestimate* the belief that people will feel inconvenienced.[7]

When applying to colleges, I had my heart set on Duke University in North Carolina. I wore the famous blue sweatshirt everywhere, I cheered for the Blue Devils basketball team, and I told anyone who would listen that it was my dream school. I was inspired by a family friend who was an alumnus and loved his experience there. A letter of recommendation from him would go a long way to helping me get in. I agonized for weeks over whether I should ask him. I even began to rationalize why I shouldn't. *He's a busy man—he won't have the time . . . Asking him would signal that I'm weak . . . Besides, I don't want to impose.*

That was the thought that plagued me the most—the idea that a favor for me would be an imposition on him. My parents tried to convince me otherwise, but I was resolute. The risk of humiliation or embarrassment was too great. And yet I wanted to go to Duke more than anything.

It was a big mistake, too, because I applied and got rejected. As things turned out, I ended up being accepted to a great school, Pepperdine in Malibu, but I was always left wondering, *What if I had gotten into Duke?*

Years later at a family brunch, I joked with that family friend about being too embarrassed to ask for his help. He didn't laugh. "Kim, it's a shame you didn't ask," he said. "I would've gladly written you a recommendation." Then he shared a quote I'll never forget:

"The pain of discomfort lasts seconds, but the pain of regret lasts a lifetime."

I look back on my 17-year-old self and see how I denied myself an opportunity, based on nothing more than *an imagined* scenario of what *I feared* someone would say. I didn't even try. That conversation with our family friend taught me an invaluable lesson. It's crucial to success to have the courage to ask for help; more often than not, people want to help.

Personally, I've found that helping people brings me joy, knowing that I've positively impacted someone else's life. Whether it's writing a recommendation, making an introduction, or giving advice to a new entrepreneur, each act of help makes me feel good.

So the next time you are weighing whether to ask someone for support, a referral, or a favor, and your mind starts inventing worries about being an imposition, remind yourself that you are on the cusp of an unknown opportunity. You aren't going to know where it leads until you move through the discomfort of asking. It might well lead nowhere. The person might not be able to help. But the point is that you've knocked on the door to see if it opens . . . leaving no room for what-ifs.

Fear of Vulnerability

When I started my first company, I often felt lost and overwhelmed, constantly worrying whether I would fail and how my friends and family would perceive me if I didn't succeed. I kept these insecurities to myself, which only intensified the stress and loneliness. If anything, I let those insecurities fuel me, working around the clock to outrun the prospect of failure. On the outside, no one had any idea what I was battling.

Eventually, I burned out. It not only took a toll on my health but also stunted my company's growth. My fear of vulnerability led me to isolate myself. I was convinced it was better to maintain a polished, professional appearance while keeping the behind-the-scenes chaos hidden away. Such thinking stemmed from a mistaken notion that the areas where we are not naturally strong or expert are weaknesses, and weaknesses are "bad." Everyone has weaknesses. More importantly, recognizing our weaknesses enables us to make key improvements, such as those crucial hires to my kitchen table! My fear of letting anyone in—of being vulnerable—had only made my situation worse.

Eventually, I came to realize that the ability to be vulnerable is a fundamental part of being human. There's strength in sharing your vulnerability with other people, because it allows them to feel safe sharing their own. Vulnerability in a leadership setting is especially important because it cultivates trust, better collaboration, and stronger teams.[8]

The ability to be vulnerable is an underrated skill set. When you are able to be vulnerable, you will be viewed as someone who is authentic. Someone capable of expressing emotion. If you are going to take people with you on your journey, being open and honest about who you are and what you are experiencing will foster a transparency that benefits everyone.

Fear of Rejection

In 2013, I was the CEO of Adconion Direct during one of the toughest markets I had ever encountered. Investors were cautious, capital was scarce, and scaling without outside investment was nearly impossible. As CEO, I had to face a harsh reality: Without fresh capital our business would grind to a halt. With just nine months of cash left in the bank, securing an investor became critical, but it wasn't just about finding any investor—we needed a strategic partner who could help us scale internationally.

Fast-forward to 2014: I received an acquisition offer from Amobee, the digital division of Singtel (Singapore Telecommunications). What caught my attention wasn't just their incredibly impressive market position and their vision for bringing our technology to Asia. There was another aspect of this potential deal that struck a deeply personal chord with me: Singtel's CEO was a woman, and their executive team was predominantly female. For the first time in my career, I wasn't going to be the only C-level woman in the room.

The deal with Singtel dragged on for months longer than we budgeted, and our cash reserves were running dangerously low. We didn't even have enough to cover payroll, and the future of Adconion hung in the balance. Without immediate funding, we risked losing everything before the acquisition could be completed. We had to raise money fast to keep Adconion afloat.

Names of investors, friends, and other relatives ran through my mind, but the idea of being rejected by the people closest to me felt humiliating. Asking for money felt extra perilous because it would reveal that my company was having cash-flow issues. I wasn't only asking them to invest in Adconion; I was also asking them to invest in me. I delayed asking for as long as possible, wondering who to ask, and how to ask, and whether to ask at all. But I was desperate, and that desperation turned on a lightbulb in my head. *What's the worst that can happen? They can only say "no."*

After rehearsing my lines like an actor, I worked up the courage to make those phone calls. To start with, I made it clear that I, too, would be investing millions of my own money into the bridge loan. "I wouldn't ask you to invest anywhere I'm not investing myself," I said. "And with these favorable terms, you'll be able to double your money in under six months."

It was a confident pitch. I felt good about it. And I was met with a resounding "No" across the board. Everyone said "Don't take it personally," but how could I not? It felt like no one believed in me. The consensus was that the investment felt too risky because "You can't guarantee the deal will close." A few of them wondered whether I was making a mistake by investing my own money. I won't lie: The collective skepticism stung. Rejection hurts, no matter how confident you are.

But I refused to allow those initial rejections to deter me. I drew up another list of names, and I made more calls. Eventually, I found a few investors who believed in the opportunity and provided the funds we needed to close the deal. I felt a commitment to them, and to myself, to prove I could close the deal despite the doubters. And guess what—121 days later, the deal closed.

Amobee, Singtel's digital division, acquired Adconion Direct for $235 million.

The biggest sale of my career—a number so large it didn't feel real.

Just six years earlier, I'd been ecstatic—on cloud nine—when I sold Frontline for $20 million! But here I was signing a deal for 10 times that amount! The number still gives me goosebumps.

It was a transformative milestone, professionally as well as personally. Once the sale was finalized, I finally had the opportunity to work alongside the women on the executive team at Singtel who'd inspired me so profoundly during the acquisition process.

I remember walking into early meetings with a mix of awe, curiosity, and pure enthusiasm. It's not every day you get the chance to learn from seasoned executives at a publicly traded company—worlds away from where I started at my kitchen table in Hawaii. I had rarely had the opportunity to work with women in leadership positions, and when I did there was usually just one. But here I was working with a team of four women who were not just leading but *thriving* in an industry dominated by men. Their mentorship was invaluable. Their approach to business prioritized long-term growth and predictable revenue—a stark contrast to my previous startup mindset, where every decision was driven by meeting this year's revenue target.

It's rare to find yourself in a room where you're both giving and growing. These women were trailblazers, and being around them was a powerful reminder of what's possible. I still carry the lessons I learned from those incredible women, whose leadership, resilience, and vision continue to inspire me.

Years later, the same friends who had turned me down admitted they regretted not investing, calling it a huge mistake. But their rejection provided me with another priceless lesson: Rejection, or the fear of it, isn't a reason to stop pursuing your dreams. It is merely a redirection to somewhere, someone, or something else. You will experience rejection. Guaranteed. But there will come a day when you'll look back and see why a particular rejection was critical to your success.

So when you're feeling nervous about a request for help you've made, remember that rejection is a natural part of life. Embracing rejection can empower you to keep pushing forward, knowing that each "no" is bringing you closer to the "yes" you are seeking.

Banishing the Lone Wolf

When you look at the four fears around asking for help, one or all of them often fuel the lone-wolf syndrome. My wolf was created in childhood and continued to haunt me into adulthood.

Early in my career, I mistakenly believed that accepting help while working toward a goal diminished my personal achievements and would make me appear less capable. This thinking was further fueled by the romanticized myth of the struggling solopreneur who reaches the top through their own hard work. I viewed help as a crutch or a prop, something to temporarily bolster me when weak, injured, or not up to the task. But the truth is quite the opposite—help isn't a prop; it's a propellant!

I can confidently say that I've exponentially increased my success by learning how to ask for help. It has allowed me to leverage my resources, amplify my strengths, and make all my assets work harder and better. It's not some big secret. As a culture, we have to remove the shame around seeking support. No one reaches the top alone— every successful person has had help along the way.

If I had known all this much earlier, I would have asked for help sooner and would have gotten farther faster. Instead, I made things harder than necessary, keeping one foot on the accelerator and the other one firmly on the brake. Now I see that trying to do everything myself was as absurd as trying to put on a one-person show, playing every part, building the set, writing the script, selling tickets, directing the orchestra, and sweeping the floor after the performance.

In most situations, we're more powerful and capable with a full cast and production crew. The same goes for family life. There's no way I could do it alone. With four kids under 10, it takes the support of my husband, family, and friends to make it all work.

If you continue to find it challenging to ask for help, try looking at it through a different lens. Think of it as gathering and leveraging resources to amplify your efforts. That way, you are taking strategic steps to make sure things are done right, allowing more room for opportunity, progress, and growth. If you can look at seeking help through a positive lens, you can put yourself in a position of strength. With that in mind, here's some guidance.

Proactively Seeking Help

When asking for help, be specific about why you are reaching out and clearly explain why you want their help. This demonstrates your thoughtfulness and respect for their time and advice. Here's an example email.

> Dear [Name],
>
> I greatly admire your experience in [insert field] and would love to learn more about your journey to success. I am working on a [insert project], and your guidance would be invaluable to me. I know you're busy, and I will make myself available to accommodate your schedule. Please let me know what works best for you.
>
> With gratitude,
> [Your Name]

If the person you approach doesn't reply, don't let that deter you. When people reach out to me and I don't reply immediately, it's not because I don't want to help. I might be super busy with a deal and their email falls through the cracks, which is why I always appreciate it when someone follows up. So, if you don't hear back, try reaching out again by email after a few days, or via text or phone, or drop by in person if they are local.

Many people give up after a single email, but I follow the "triple tap" approach—send an email, follow up, and follow up again. If you still don't get a response after three attempts, move on to someone else who will be more likely to help.

Always ask yourself how important or valuable it is to get help from a particular person. Examine *why* they've come to mind. If you truly believe their help could make a difference, then by all means make a trip to see them in person. It might be the most expensive cup of coffee or lunch you've ever had, but the result could be priceless. I do this all the time. I tell someone that "I will be in your area on a specific week, my schedule is flexible, and I would love to meet up." By making it convenient for them to meet, people are far more likely to say "yes."

In fact, one of the pieces of advice I share often with ambitious and aspiring leaders is: "Ask your way to success."

Ask for help.

Ask for advice.

Ask for the sale.

Ask for a mentor.

If you don't ASK, you're not going to GET.

Be bold. Have courage. Ask for what you want.

Just like a 12-year-old Steve Jobs once did. He cold-called the co-founder of Hewlett Packard after searching for his number in the telephone book.[9] Jobs was a high school student building a frequency counter and figured Bill Hewlett would have some spare parts lying around. Not only did Hewlett send him the parts, he also offered Jobs a summer job on the assembly line. "I just asked," Jobs later reflected.

"Most people never ask. And that's what separates the people that do things from the people who just dream about them. You gotta act."

Once I began asking, my life changed exponentially. I moved from working solo late into the night to collaborating with a team every day. From that point on, I was never afraid to ask for help. I've seen the value in raising my hand or making a call, whether it's for assistance from a team member, problem-solving with a fellow entrepreneur, or calling a friend to bounce some ideas around. And the relationships I've built along the way with peers, colleagues, and mentors have been instrumental to my journey. Success isn't about having all the answers, it's about knowing when to ask for help.

LESSON IN THE MISTAKE

Embrace collaboration, seek
guidance, and ask for help.
No one is successful alone.

CHAPTER SUMMARY

Self-reflection: What fear is preventing you from asking for help? What skills do you lack that other people could provide? Imagine what would be possible if you weren't doing everything yourself.

Key Takeaways:

▶ **The Lone-Wolf Mentality Is a Dangerous Trap:** The most successful people in the world achieved their goals through collaboration and support from others. Banish the lone-wolf mentality. You'll never reach your full potential if you try to go it alone.

▶ **Four Fears Prevent People from Asking for Help:** *Fear of judgment, fear of imposing, fear of rejection, fear of vulnerability.* These fears, while common, often create imagined barriers rather than real ones.

▶ **Asking for Help Is a Strength, Not a Weakness:** People consistently underestimate others' willingness to help. Adopt the triple-tap approach—ask, follow up, follow up again.

▶ **Embrace Vulnerable Leadership:** The ability to be vulnerable and open cultivates trust, better collaboration, and stronger teams. Be authentic. Be human. Colleagues and employees will follow your lead.

▶ **Build a Strong Network:** Building a strong network of mentors, peers, and colleagues can be a game changer. Surround yourself with supportive, inspiring individuals who demand you live up to your greatest potential.

Millionaire Mindset: Success is a team effort, and no one achieves greatness alone. I will ask my way to success. I invite collaboration, connection, and assistance to help me grow.

Being Paralyzed by Fear of Failure

Here's what nobody tells you about becoming a millionaire:
The biggest obstacle isn't the market, the competition, or
even a lack of capital—it's the war between your dreams
and your fears. The worst mistake you can make isn't failing.
It's fearing failure so much that you don't take risks.

The meatball almost rolled off my fork. "Wait, what? You want us to talk about the *worst* thing that happened to us today?" I stared at my dad, baffled, across the dinner table. "Are you serious?"

In most families, spaghetti night means talking about school projects, sports games, or upcoming birthdays. You know, normal kid stuff. But in my house, dinner conversations were different. From a young age, my parents started to talk about failure, and this became a nightly ritual to see who racked up the most losses.

My dad didn't let my siblings and me avoid the topic. "Go on, what's the worst thing that happened to you today? Kimmy, you first," he said, smiling.

I sighed. It felt embarrassing, but I knew we wouldn't be able to leave the table without playing his game. "Well, my math teacher gave us a pop quiz and I didn't understand any of it."

My parents nodded and listened kindly as we took turns sharing the worst part of our day. Most people think it's taboo to talk about failure. But in my family? Failures became a normal part of dinner, passed around the table like salt. And so this became our dinner ritual: sharing the day's failures like they were highlights from a sports game. Missed school buses. Forgetting homework. My crush asking my best friend to the school dance. Or that time I called my teacher "Mom"—nothing was off-limits. My dad's philosophy was simple: "You can try your best and still fail," he'd always say, waving a fork for emphasis. "But so what? Try your best, make mistakes. Failing doesn't make you a failure."

He would know. He didn't just preach failure—he lived it.

His first business was a self-service auto repair garage that let people rent tools and fix their own cars, but that flopped because nobody wanted to fix their own cars. I still remember being in my childhood bedroom, hearing my parents' tense whispers about how we were going to pay the mortgage. But my dad was famous for saying, "Don't worry, I'll find a way." It was almost like if he said it enough times, it would miraculously come true.

His next "visionary idea" was to devise and create a machine that made roofing tiles. The idea had everything going for it, but then the housing market bottomed out and no one was building, so that failed, too. Now my parents' arguing echoed through the house. My dad treated failure like whack-a-mole: When one business was struck down, another would pop up. He went on to open a steakhouse, an internet cafe, and a neighborhood dive bar. All went belly-up, so what did he decide to do next? Open a laundromat. And when the laundromat started to struggle, he came up with the "creative solu-tion" of adding a sandwich kiosk next to the dryer machines, but that didn't fix the problem. Failure never stopped him. It fueled him. He'd just pick himself up and chase after the next dream. He'd wink at me and say, "Don't worry, Kimmy, one day my luck will change."

As much as I wanted to believe him, my siblings and I could feel the tension rising in our household after every failure. I'd lie in bed wondering: *Was the whole purpose behind the dinner ritual of sharing failures less about learning life lessons and more about justifying my dad's growing list of failures?* Through my childhood eyes, all it did was cre-ate animosity and instability.

Growing up, my siblings and I developed a "failure radar"—that sixth sense that warns you of trouble before it arrives. We could sense the mounting pressure in our home after each setback. We knew it was bad the day our heat was turned off in the dead of winter. One unpaid electric bill wasn't a crisis in my dad's eyes—he just made us put on more layers to stay warm. For him, a crisis was not being able to make the mortgage payment, and he came perilously close to that out-come many times. My dad's philosophy—"If you're not failing, you're not on the road to success!"—didn't bring much comfort as we wore turtlenecks and jackets to bed.

But here's the plot twist that would've made 10-year-old me drop my meatball—by the time I got to college, my dad had finally struck gold. He made millions in the real estate business, buying distressed properties after the market crashed, fixing them up, and holding them. By the time I turned 20, he had more than 100 rental houses. After years of setbacks, he ultimately built his fortune on his failures. That taught me an undeniable fact—success takes time, and in his case, decades.

If you're not prepared to fail, you're not prepared to become a millionaire.

Success demands resilience and the willingness to get back up, no matter how many times you fall. But knowing this doesn't make the fear vanish or feel any less scary. Just because meteorologists warn about a Category 5 hurricane barreling toward the coast, it doesn't make the storm any less frightening. You can brace yourself, but that doesn't mean it won't hurt when it hits. Even though my dad did his best to prepare us for setbacks, nothing truly equipped me for the moment I had to face my first real failure head-on.

In 2010, after selling my first company, I finally had the capital to invest in new opportunities. Up to this point, I hadn't invested in anything, so actually having enough money to meaningfully invest was a major milestone in my life, and I had the ego to think I'd be a natural.

At that time, the online subscription model was booming. New startups were emerging everywhere, introducing monthly memberships in jewelry, beauty, wine, flowers, fashion, and more. ShoeDazzle, co-founded by Kim Kardashian, was at the forefront of the trend, with millions of consumers eagerly embracing subscription-based shopping. Amazon had also acquired Zappos for $1.2 billion in 2009, reinforcing the idea that creating a marketplace for buying shoes online was a massive opportunity. So, I decided to capitalize on the emerging trend and start a new company with two friends, both seasoned entrepreneurs.

We created Shoe Privée, a monthly subscription service where members received a stylish new pair of shoes, handpicked by fashion experts, each month for only $39.95. It seemed like a recipe for success: women love shoes, the price was unbeatable, and you didn't have to leave your house to go shopping. Plus, my co-founders and I were serial entrepreneurs. What could go wrong?

Everything.

The cracks started to show early. Customers were excited for the first few months, but then reality hit: They didn't actually want 12 new pairs of shoes every year. I can remember walking into the office one day and seeing shoe boxes stacked in towering, wobbly columns—a perfect symbol of how badly we had miscalculated demand.

Then, the financial strain kicked in. The cost of acquiring customers was sky-high in such a competitive space. We were spending way too much on marketing and not bringing in enough revenue per member to justify it. On top of that, inventory was mounting so we switched to quarterly shipments. However, that reduced our monthly sales and accelerated our losses. We kept trying, desperately iterating—we pivoted to men's shoes, changed the price point, dropped the membership fees—but ultimately nothing worked.

Within just a few short years, we had no choice but to shut down all operations.

I lost everything I had invested—hundreds of thousands of dollars.

I was devastated. Shoe Privée wasn't just a financial failure—it was a personal one. And that's when fear took over. This is what fear does: It floods the mind, creates an overload of self-defeating thoughts, and undermines your confidence to the point where you feel stuck. I let fear paralyze me. This paralysis showed up in seemingly small ways at first. When a former colleague asked me to invest in a new digital advertising startup, a space where I was an expert, I stalled. I kept using the stalling tactic of "I need to think about it," until the round closed without me. Then, an investor I deeply respected approached me about a cutting-edge ad-tech startup, something firmly in my wheelhouse, and I passed—not because it wasn't a great opportunity, but because I no longer trusted myself to pick a winner.

The paralysis spread like emotional quicksand. The more I wrestled with it, the deeper I sank into immobility. I stayed put on the sidelines, watching countless deals unfold before my eyes, paralyzed by the thought of making another wrong move. Fear is a complicated compass. While it may point you toward safety, it will never lead you to greatness. My mistake wasn't just listening to what fear had to say; it was trusting it as the only voice of reason.

A few years later, I found myself sitting back at my parents' dinner table for Thanksgiving. There's something about being in your childhood home that instantly makes you feel like a kid again. Our dinner routine had barely changed, but this time I wasn't the nervous kid sharing small school mishaps. I was a grown woman who had built and lost businesses, who had tasted success and had her fair share of failure.

At one point during dinner, as we passed around the mashed potatoes, I casually mentioned a new venture I had considered investing in but didn't. "I just couldn't pull the trigger," I admitted. "Shoe Privée still lingers in my mind. I don't fully trust myself yet."

My dad set down his fork and said, "Kimmy, don't let fear of failure hold you back from taking risks."

His words landed like a gut punch. It was the same lesson he had tried to instill in us at the dinner table all those years ago. The same principle that had propelled him through countless failures before he finally struck gold. And yet, there I was, letting failure define me.

That moment flipped a switch in me. Fear had paralyzed me from taking action for too long. It was time to stop letting it dictate my decisions. Because if there's one thing my dad knew better than anyone else, it was this: The only true failure is to stop trying.

Failure doesn't have to be paralyzing. No one has reached success without overcoming a mental obstacle or without needing the tenacity to create, launch, build, and bounce back from setbacks. Successful people don't allow fear to dictate their choices. So the key is to not dismiss or disregard fear but instead move through it, as if walking through a dense, eerie blanket of fog.

I always tell ambitious, success-driven people: "Be the buffalo!" That usually gets me a few weird looks, but hear me out.

When a storm approaches, most animals instinctively flee, trying to outrun the danger. But buffalo take a different approach. They charge directly into the storm. By doing so, they're able to get through the storm quicker than if they tried to escape. It's a powerful metaphor for resilience, highlighting how confronting a challenge head-on can lead to better outcomes.

The 3 AM Wake-Up Call

The fear of failure still wakes me up at 3 AM.

It arrives in the form of a recurring nightmare where my company is on the brink of failing. I wake up, heart racing, body sweating, my stomach in knots.

I know exactly what's happening—deep down, I'm still haunted by the fear of repeating a failure like Shoe Privée. Even when you move past fear, it doesn't mean it disappears forever. Fear lingers, always lurking beneath the surface. And it's often irrational. But the difference is that now I no longer let fear stop me; I move forward despite it.

Fear is a survival instinct that doesn't distinguish between real threats and imagined ones. Our brain sees them as the same. The amygdala—the tiny almond-shaped part of the brain that governs our emotions and triggers fear—can't differentiate between a very present danger (a tiger in the bushes) and a self-created fear (the possibility of a company failing). Think of your amygdala as your emotional smoke detector: It will go off as loudly for an imagined disaster scenario as it will for a real one. It's firing the same "BEWARE!" alert because that's what it's programmed to do, to protect us from imminent danger. It's why most people often choose the safe option of not taking a risk—safety equals survival.

But a millionaire mindset has to overcome this instinctual response, because true success requires dancing with uncertainty. You can't reach extraordinary heights without venturing beyond your comfort zone. To make it big, you have to be willing to take a risk.

It's usually right before we take a leap into the unknown that fear of failure sneaks in, disguised as what-ifs, seeding just enough doubt that sometimes you choose not to do anything at all. Because it feels safer. The higher the stakes, the louder the fear.

What if it doesn't work?

What if I'm seen as a failure?

What if I'm not good enough?

What if people judge me?

What if I regret making this decision?

In all cases, it's an *imagined* outcome. An *imagined* ridicule. An *imagined* embarrassment. That's the power of fear. Or, I should say, that's the power of the mind.

Aviation pioneer Amelia Earhart said it best. "The most difficult thing to do is the decision to act. Think of your fears as paper tigers. You can do anything you decide to do. You can act to change and control your life; the procedure, the process is its own reward."

The fears are paper tigers—a great reminder about the illusion fears create. They are not as difficult to overcome as you might initially think. Only when you take action do you realize how easily the illusion dissolves.

Of course, fear is not a bad thing. It serves a purpose aside from protection. It's also a reminder of the risks involved, an opportunity to pause and double-check your plan. But fear alone should not be the reason you don't move forward. It only becomes problematic when fear stops you from acting and executing by generating some familiar

excuses: *The timing isn't right . . . I need to sit with this a little longer . . .*
I'll wait until I'm 100% ready.

So how can you get out of your own way? What are the practical
steps that will bring you out of fear paralysis? I use a three-step process that works for me every time—understand the fear, acknowledge
the fear, and push past the fear.

Step 1: Understand the Fear

Instead of allowing fear to send you into a spiral, take a step back to
examine what's really going on. Why is your fear so strong? What's
the "story" behind it?

When you figure out the "why," you bring the analytical mind
into the same space that fear occupies, and fear doesn't like to hang
out with reason and knowledge. It's like turning on the lights when
you're frightened of a shadow in your bedroom. Once your analytical
brain shows up to the party, you realize there's no monster lurking in
the corner.

My fear of failure has resurfaced many times in my life—when I
thought I'd get evicted after getting fired, when I doubted my decision to launch my first business, and when I was scared to invest again
after Shoe Privée failed.

Let's face it, there is always a distinct possibility of failure. I'd
watched my dad risk everything and, time and time again, I found
myself stepping into the same uncertainty I once swore I'd avoid. But
throughout my career, knowing where the fear stemmed from helped
me trust my intuition and vision *more than* my fear.

Whether it's a waking fear or one programmed into the subconscious, it still helps to understand what is hindering your progress.
So take a pen and paper and bring some objective curiosity to your
fear of failure. Below, I've given an example of the questions to ask,

using sample answers from my own experience before I started my first company:

> **What am I afraid of?** *My new business failing.*
>
> **Why am I feeling this way?** *Because I'm about to launch my own company for the first time, I've borrowed money from Nanny, and there's a lot of uncertainty ahead.*
>
> **What is this experience reminding me of?** *The time when I was growing up and I watched my father start a new business with lots of enthusiasm and seeing it fail years later.*
>
> **What's the story I've built around this fear?** *That failure is part of my DNA. That I will never succeed.*

By writing down these kinds of observations, you're taking proactive steps toward dismantling the fear and building the strength to look it in the eye.

Step 2: Acknowledge the Fear

Once you understand what's going on, it's time to acknowledge, accept, and accommodate the fear itself. Naming fears transforms them from a general, undefined anxiety into something tangible. Dr. Dan Siegel's "name it to tame it" method is a simple way to label your fear and make it feel less overwhelming.

For example, maybe you're thinking *I'm going to fail.* Or *I'm not good enough.* Or *I'm going to get laughed at.* Now name them clearly: fear of failure, fear of being underqualified, fear of ridicule. Once the fear is named, ask yourself this: "Is it true?"

In other words, is there factual evidence that what you're fearing is true or actually happening? If the fear is "A bear is going to kill me" and you are literally faced with a bear on a hiking trail, then, yes, it's true, and you'll act accordingly with survival in mind. But if the fear is "I'm not good enough" and you haven't even started, then the fear is most likely false.

So when a fear pops into your mind, taking a pause to ask if it's true can provide perspective. That's why "naming it to tame it" is such a helpful exercise, because you are essentially building a case against imagined scenarios. You're deliberately using the logical part of the mind to override the emotional reactivity that whips up worst-case scenarios.

It makes perfect sense that psychologists have found that simply recognizing our fears makes them easier to handle. Kristy Dalrymple, an assistant professor of psychiatry and human behavior at Brown University, says, "The more you try to suppress fear—either by ignoring it or doing something else to displace it—the more you will actually experience it."[10]

And Leon Hoffman, co-director of the Pacella Research Center in New York, says there is a benefit to facing this challenging emotion. "Showing fear is considered to be a weakness. But you are actually stronger if you can acknowledge fear."[11]

When you learn to rationalize why you're in the grip of fear—be it a nightmare, the imagination, or a lingering memory from the past—the sense of fear tends to diminish. I used this method to overcome my fear of flying. I felt the fear in my white knuckles and creeping sense of panic as the plane doors closed, but I closed my eyes, felt all the sensations, and then rationalized how thousands of planes take off every single day from hundreds of airports around the world; and how, statistically, I'm more likely to die in a car crash than a plane crash. I felt the fear but never let it stop me from getting on a flight.

So get into the habit of naming your fears and rationalizing why they don't make sense. It's similar to what my dad did when he asked about the worst thing that happened in our day—you're getting comfortable with fear and reducing its power over you.

Step 3: Move Through the Fear

Now it's time to be the buffalo. Because fear is not just a feeling, it's a decision point.

I'm not pretending that it's easy to dive headfirst into your fear, but my guess is that you're braver and more capable than you give yourself credit for. In fact, recall a time when you last had a fear but proceeded anyway. It could be a big or small moment. Most people who consider this question come to realize they've already overcome fear in the past. If that's the case for you, how can you use the lessons learned to move through whatever you're facing today?

It took me many years before I learned how to skillfully move through my fears. They still come up and still rattle me. But I refuse to stay stuck in fear. Like any skill, it requires practice. But from first-hand experience, I can tell you it's incredibly freeing to feel the fear and act anyway!

When you do take the leap, be prepared for the critics. People have a habit of reminding you of the risks, telling you not to be reckless, even doubting your abilities. Don't let anyone else's critiques stop you from pursuing your dreams. It's easy to stand on the sidelines and judge without taking risks. I love the passage from a famous speech Theodore Roosevelt delivered in Paris called "Man in the Arena," praising those who have the courage to take action regardless of the critics.[12]

> *It is not the critic who counts; not the man who points out how the strong man stumbles or where the doer of deeds could have done better. The credit belongs to the man who is actually in the arena, whose face is marred by dust and sweat and blood; who strives valiantly; who errs and comes up short again and again, because there is no effort without error or shortcoming; but who knows the*

*great enthusiasms, the great devotions; who spends himself in a
worthy cause; who, at the best, knows, in the end, the triumph of
high achievement, and who, at the worst, if he fails, at least he fails
while daring greatly, so that his place shall never be with those cold
and timid souls who knew neither victory nor defeat.*

Confronting your fears takes a deep inner strength. And if it's not
strength, then it's the sheer intolerance of the prospect of life staying
the same, as illustrated by the story of an Uber driver who picked me
up at Los Angeles International Airport.

Isaac had spent 15 years on the East Coast working in IT for
different companies, but, at the age of 35, with a wife and two children, he couldn't shake the desire to run his own business one day
and escape the harsh winters of Boston. The fear of letting down his
family had kept him frozen in a monotonous yet stable corporate job.
After summoning the courage to take the leap, he quit, and he and his
family moved to California. He was moonlighting as an Uber driver
to earn a steady income so he could fulfill his dream of starting a con-
struction company by day.

I admired his courage. "What made you jump?"

"I couldn't bear another day doing what I was doing," he said. "I
figured the risk of going for it was not as great as the risk to my mental
health if I stayed doing a job I hated."

"I respect your fearlessness!" I said.

He laughed. "I have more fears now than ever. But with a year's
worth of savings, I have a one-year runway to figure things out. My
wife and I sat down and had a real conversation about how to make
this work for our family."

He felt the fear but took action anyway . . . because he had assessed
the risk of inaction. Waking up in a year's time and being in the exact
same place felt like a surefire way to continue feeling unfulfilled.

The risk of standing still is far greater than the risk of moving forward.

Ask yourself: "How would I feel if I'm still in the same position 12 months from now?"

Isaac had a game plan to save enough resources before quitting his job. But the most important part was that he took action. I've said it before, though it's always worth repeating: Don't be afraid to take that first step. Keep your eyes on the prize and MOVE. If necessary, have a contingency plan, create a Plan B, and know when to pivot. But what a travesty it would be to look back on your life and see regrets instead of the risks you're glad you took.

When faced with a hard decision, will you let fear stop you, or will you be the buffalo? Choose the path driven by your vision, not your fears. Embrace the storm and live the life you imagine.

Redefining Success Through Failure

Failure isn't something they teach in school, but it should be. If it had been, my dad would have been a world-famous professor with his "What's the worst that can happen?" mindset.

From an early age, most of us are raised with a singular focus on success. Is it any wonder we're not good at failing? But it's my hope that as a society we learn to embrace failure, to demystify it and peel back the shame, to acknowledge that in order to achieve success we must risk failing. And by inviting risk, we also open ourselves to the possibility of making mistakes.

Throughout my career, I've had my fair share of failures. If they issued diplomas in the field of failure, I'd have an undergraduate degree, a master's, and a couple of doctorates. And you know what? I'd frame each one and hang it proudly on my wall. Because each setback and failing—even the events that felt like a disaster at the time—made me *better*. I learned. I grew. I became smarter. To this day, when something doesn't go right, I like to examine where it went wrong and what I could do differently next time. If you are truly prepared to learn from failure, it can only improve your performance and productivity.

Few have embraced failure as courageously as Elon Musk, especially in the early days of SpaceX when he faced a relentless series of setbacks. Rocket after rocket exploded, and many people thought his efforts were doomed. But Musk continued to launch, test, and learn. He embraced failure as a critical component of innovation and progress.

"Failure is an option here. If things are not failing, you are not innovating enough," he famously said in an interview. Musk's openness to failing is a powerful reminder that great breakthroughs often come not despite failure but because of it.

In the same way that fear can ignite the what-ifs that push you toward safety, your passion and sense of purpose can fuel your determination to keep pushing forward. So keep reminding yourself of what first motivated you to pursue something new. That initial reason will provide a solid anchor to combat any emotional reactivity. Being crystal clear about your vision keeps you focused, no matter what challenges come up. It's your North Star—the guiding light that directs you toward your dreams.

Kobe Bryant exemplifies the mastery of failure like no one else. His renowned "Mamba mentality" is the athletic equivalent of a millionaire mindset. I've heard many psychologists refer to the same defining moment in his career—the 1997 NBA Western Conference semifinals. At the time, 18-year-old Kobe was a rising star and, in a game broadcast on national TV, the Lakers and the Utah Jazz were tied 89–89 in a fifth-game clincher, with overtime ticking down. Kobe received the ball in almost perfect scoring positions four times. But he shot four airballs. Each missed shot led to howls of disbelief in the arena—and those costly misses were viewed as one of the great playoff failures.

Afterward, Kobe sat courtside, with his head buried in his hands. A reporter later asked him what he had been feeling at that moment. Kobe seemed confused. "Feeling? What's *feeling* got to do with it? I was working out why I shot four airballs." The emotions of the failure didn't concern him. His sole focus was learning for the next game.

Michael Jordan also exemplified the same pursuit of excellence. His mindset viewed every missed shot as just another shot closer to victory. In the docuseries *The Last Dance*, he talks about what he learned from his failures. "I've missed more than nine thousand shots in my career. I've lost almost three hundred games. Twenty-six times, I've been trusted to take the game-winning shot . . . and missed. I've failed over and over and over again. And that is why I succeed."

Whatever dream or goal you're pursuing, you owe it to yourself to bring a similar level of discipline, willpower, and desire to learn. From personal experience, I know my failure is directly correlated to my success. I also know from conversations with other successful people that mistakes were an essential part of their growth and success, too.

There is no such thing as a risk-free life. But that is not something to fear; it is something to embrace. So when failure visits, put out the welcome mat. It is going to lead you toward opportunity and growth and, along the way, you will see how much you adapt, evolve, and ultimately learn. Two basketball greats are proof that failure isn't your enemy; it's your teacher.

Conquering Your Inner Critic

How do you talk to yourself? If we could somehow listen to each other's thoughts, I suspect we'd be shocked by what we hear. That's because we are usually our own harshest critics. Our self-talk is often unkind, unforgiving, and judgmental. That's why conquering the doubt of your inner voice is one of the most crucial steps when it comes to overcoming fear.

Consider this: We each have a personal narrator working 24/7 to provide commentary on every thought, emotion, interaction, decision, and possibility. In most cases, that narrator has some serious opinions—it loves to offer unsolicited feedback on every mistake, setback, and failure. And it shapes how you see yourself and the world around you. The content and impact of those stories you tell yourself depends on whether you indulge negative self-talk or encourage positive self-talk. Or, as I like to see it, whether you invite the inner critic or the inner cheerleader.

When it comes to the fear of failure, that voice is the difference between being paralyzed by inaction and being motivated to take the risk to make your dreams come true.

When I was in my early 20s, I sold men's suits at Nordstrom. This was my first sales job, and I felt shy and unsure of myself. I can remember walking into my first day with such trepidation, trying to sound strong and confident (when I felt the total opposite). Back then, my inner voice was a tiny gremlin perched on my shoulder, seeding doubt, crushing my confidence: *You're not good enough to be doing this job*, it whispered. *People are going to notice your inexperience . . . You don't have what it takes . . . You'll never be able to do this.*

The inner critic was my default setting.

Until I realized that I had the power to tune it out.

A few weeks later, having landed a few customers, I realized that I had a natural knack for sales. I also realized that the tone and content of my inner dialogue was up to me. Did I want my life to be narrated by the inner critic or the inner cheerleader?

For some people, the inner critic can be loud and fierce, forever scolding them for every mistake. If you have a fear of failure, it will bring out the megaphone. That's why I asked about how you talk to yourself. It's important to become aware of the nature of this self-talk.

Andy Puddicombe, former Buddhist monk and co-founder of the Headspace meditation app, says: "It's only when we pay attention to our inner dialogue that we see how hard we can be on ourselves. Ask yourself, 'If you spoke the same way to a close friend, how would they react?' The answer often provides a fair idea of how much kinder you need to be to yourself, offering the same kind of understanding and encouragement you'd give that friend."

Once we become aware of the inner dialogue playing in our minds, we can begin to use it to our advantage. Since the mind will keep chattering away, why not ensure its words are positive and empowering?

Our capacity to believe the fear of failure is equal to our capacity to overcome it.

"I am not good enough" can become "I am more than capable."

"I'm going to fail" can become "This is going to be a huge success."

Your entire daily attitude can be: "I'm powerful . . . I'm extraordinary . . . I can do this!"

By incorporating more positive self-talk, you have an effective antidote to fear. It's why I have a bulletin board of positive messages in my bathroom that I read every morning and every night, soaking up what the inner cheerleader has to say. Positive self-talk is a daily practice. The more you do it, the better you get.

Here's an exercise to ensure that your inner voice is cheering you on, not finding fault:

List five qualities about yourself. For example, are you creative, curious, generous, resourceful? If you have a hard time thinking what your qualities might be, ask a friend or close family member what they would say about you.

Next, write down five positive things about the goal you want to achieve (why it's going to make a difference, why it's unique, why you deserve it, why it will work out, etc.).

Finally, write down five things in life that you're most grateful for (a person, a place, a pet, an opportunity).

Reflecting on the good things cultivates a positive state of mind, and I would encourage you to practice this exercise at least once a week. If you can get used to speaking to yourself in a positive, upbeat, optimistic way, you will start to feel the difference, and the fear of failure won't have anywhere to live.

Trust Your Intuition, Not Your Fears

The moment you experience fear, you're in your head, overthinking everything. It's hard to make a clear-cut decision when so many thoughts and emotions are swirling, obscuring any sense of clarity. You can only think straight when the dust has settled, the stress has been reduced, and the mind is clearer and quieter. It's in that calmer place that you also have a better chance of tuning into a superpower for its decision-making capabilities—your intuition.

I'll never be one who advocates for making snap decisions. Every big decision deserves our intellect, experience, and analytical thinking. But our intuition—an inner guidance that arrives as a hunch/nudge/feeling experienced viscerally at a core level—should be factored into the equation, too, especially when making life-changing moves.

I can't think of a time when I haven't relied on my intuition to guide me, especially when faced with daunting odds. I trusted my gut as I launched a digital advertising company even as the dot-com bubble burst, to enter the crowded beverage market with a tea brand right in the middle of a pandemic, and to start a Web3 company when the crypto market was plummeting. Each time, I overcame my fear of failure and took the leap.

Research supports the idea that trusting your gut can provide a helpful steer when there is a certain "unknowability" at play. Laura Huang, an associate professor of business administration at Harvard Business School, has researched the subject of intuition more than most. After conducting multiple studies, she found that a gut feeling is scientifically useful.

She wrote: "In several studies . . . I found that the role of gut feel is often to inspire a leader to make a call, particularly when the decision is risky. In the face of information overload, mounting risks and uncertainty, and intense pressures to make the right decisions, there is often debilitating evidence that delays our decision making. Trusting your gut allows leaders the freedom to move forward."[13]

Another reminder to never underestimate your instincts!

The mind is an incredible analytical tool that allows us to weigh, examine, process, and consider, turning the pros and cons of any situation inside out. But that doesn't mean we should ignore our intuition. How many times have you heard someone say, "I knew I should have listened to my gut!" or "I had a gut feeling but did it anyway"? It's because we *feel* something but then tend to *think* about it. And so the thinking mind—our intellect—overrides or dismisses what we feel deep down. As Laura Huang says, "If you apply logic and data to gut feel, the more likely you are to put off a decision or make a worse one."

Our intuition can make itself known on a deal, a project, a date, or a wedding day; it can be a feeling that arrives at the beach, by the river, or in the car, signaling danger ahead, long before danger is visible. For a lot of people, it's an inexplicable feeling or sensation; for others, it can arrive as a "whisper" during meditation or relaxation, or a fleeting image that comes to mind. However it arrives, an intuitive signal is always worth listening to, because it's trying to tell you something.

Steve Jobs often spoke about intuition's key role in his decision-making at Apple. Like many great innovators and inventors throughout history, he often set aside pure logic and instead trusted his gut. Jobs's outlook was shaped by a life-changing trip to India when he was 19, and its spiritual culture taught him to experiment with his intuition. "The people in the Indian countryside don't use their intellect like we do; they use their intuition," he told biographer Walter Isaacson. "Intuition is a very powerful thing, more powerful than intellect, in my opinion. That's had a big impact on my work."[14]

So it's always worth taking the time to "check in" with your gut, especially when the fear of failure is strong and present. Fearful thoughts may have already forced you to retreat or rethink, leaving you paralyzed by indecision. That's when you can call on your intuition, because it can be trusted far more than your fears.

You know a "NO!" when you *feel* it. You know a "HELL YES!" when you feel it, too. Notice I'm saying "feel it," not "think it." Because the intuitive response is coming from deep within, not the mind. As Jobs says, the mind can be a restless place but, if you learn to calm it, "there's room to hear more subtle things—that's when your intuition starts to blossom."

Personally, when I'm faced with two choices, I experience either butterflies in my stomach or a knot in my stomach. The butterflies are accompanied by a light, energetic, uplifting feeling—that's my "yes." The knot leaves me feeling heavy, stiff, anxious, and sometimes nauseated—that's my signal something is "off." The sensations can be different for different people, but you'll grow familiar with how your intuition sends you signals.

To train your intuition, find somewhere to relax. Take a few deep, calming breaths, and then, depending on the choice before you, give yourself two options. It could be a choice of restaurants, movies at the theater, what clothes to wear, or places to visit on the weekend. Bring both options to mind and see what each one *feels* like. The intuitive hit might not come right away, but the more you practice, the more you can hone your intuition as an inner quality to consult when the fear of failure causes you to stall.

Setbacks Shape Success

Setbacks, missteps, and challenges are essential ingredients for any recipe for success. My dad was right about preparing us for that inevitability from a young age. But I've since borrowed from my friend an updated version of his "What's the worst that can happen?" ritual for my children. When we sit around the dinner table, we don't focus only on the "worst." Instead, we encourage a more well-rounded reflection. This new ritual is called "Pow, Wow, Bow"—as created by life coach Abbey Ziv. We end each day by sharing our:

- **Pow**—the worst thing that happened,
- **Wow**—the best thing that happened,
- **Bow**—something we're grateful for.

This practice highlights our struggles, celebrates our wins, and expresses gratitude. It's a reminder that life is full of ups and downs, and that our ability to adapt along the way is key. The worst might happen. The best might happen. The only thing we can control is how we respond to each twist and turn.

Today, when I start any new venture, I expect bumps in the road. I expect to make mistakes. I expect roadblocks, even failures. But I also expect to win. I expect breakthroughs and success. This mindset shift has allowed me to push forward whatever obstacles and challenges arise along the way.

I want you to try to do the same thing. Every time you stumble, or a project gets derailed, or you get rejected, remind yourself: It's not the end. Adjust your perspective to view failure as a necessary step toward achieving success.

When, like the buffalo, you charge through the storms of life with courage, you discover a resilience you never knew you had. Don't let the fear of failure hold you back. Don't get caught up in an endless loop of what-ifs. Don't let fear stand in the way of your potential for greatness. At the end of the day, the only real failure is in not trying at all.

LESSON IN THE MISTAKE

Fear doesn't prevent bad
things from happening—
it stops great things from
starting if you give it the
power to.

CHAPTER SUMMARY

Self-reflection: Is fear of failure holding you back from pursuing a goal or dream? Notice how you talk to yourself—is it positive or negative? How does your inner voice influence your decisions?

Key Takeaways:

▶ **Redefine Failure:** Failure is inevitable. Embrace it as an inevitable part of life. If you can view failure as a learning tool, every setback becomes a stepping stone toward success. Dreams that don't come true often lead to the ones that do!

▶ **Face Your Fears:** To master the art of failure, face your fears. Understand and acknowledge them to disempower them. Take the time to unpack each fear, trace its roots, and free yourself to take action.

▶ **Be the Buffalo:** Move through your fears. Be the buffalo—run into the storm and face challenges head-on. Viewing the unknown with curiosity helps you to move through difficulties faster and emerge stronger.

▶ **Trust Your Intuition:** Tune out your fears and tap into your inner guidance system. Your intuition can be trusted; your fears can't. The more you learn to listen to your intuition, the more you will be able to act on your inner knowing, rather than hesitating because of your fears. Your hunches are trying to tell you something.

▶ **"What's the Worst That Can Happen?":** The worst-case scenario often isn't as catastrophic as we imagine. Turn negative self-talk into positive self-talk. Instead of worst-case scenarios, focus on best-case scenarios. Find the reasons why you CAN do something.

▶ **Take Action Despite Fear:** Don't let fear hold you back from chasing your dreams. Remember, fears are "paper tigers" that only get stronger if you feed them. Success is found in taking action. Letting fear dictate your decisions leads to stagnation, while moving forward despite it fosters growth, opportunities, and long-term success.

Millionaire Mindset: Failure is part of the journey. I'm tenacious, resourceful, and capable of turning challenges into opportunities. Every mistake allows me to learn where I went wrong and grow.

Keeping Toxic Relationships in Your Inner Circle

Toxic relationships can do more damage than a bad business deal.
Holding on to them isn't loyalty—it's a mistake.

I can still smell the pine trees and feel the fresh breeze at the summer camp in Oregon. That's where I first met Emma. We were 12 years old and became inseparable, sharing whispered secrets in our bunk beds and making promises we swore would last forever. At least we thought they would. That's the thing about toxic relationships—they rarely start out toxic. Sometimes they begin in the happiest moments, which makes them all the harder to detect.

For years, Emma was my constant. We navigated the treacherous waters of middle school together, became each other's cheerleaders when boyfriends dumped us, and cried on each other's shoulders when parting ways for college. Even then, the physical distance couldn't separate us. We spent hours on the phone, dissecting our lives, sharing our news, and offloading our fears. When I decided to start my own company, Emma was the first person I called. I can still hear the genuine enthusiasm in her voice. "You've got this, Kim!" she said. Her belief in me was exactly what I needed to hear.

But over the years after starting my company, something shifted. It was barely noticeable at first. So subtle that I almost missed it. A doubtful comment here and a backhanded compliment there. "Ohhhh, you're working late *again*?"

With my company growing so fast, the late nights didn't feel like a sacrifice, but she nevertheless made me feel self-conscious about how hard I was working. At the time, I didn't interpret her comments as intentionally mean. After all, this was Emma—my childhood best friend, soul sister, practically family. But as the pace of growth accelerated, so did the weight of Emma's words.

I remember telling her my excitement after receiving the Ernst & Young Entrepreneur of the Year award. But instead of congratulating me, she was "shocked" that I had won. From there on out, every one of my successes was met with a condescending "Of course you did." Every time I faced a setback and reached out for sympathy, she only made me feel worse and turned it into an "I told you so" moment. I started to notice how her words affected me. Our catch-ups—once the highlight of my week—became draining and often left me feeling inadequate.

Our lives had gone in very different directions. She had stayed in the same sales job all these years and recently had her first child. When we talked, there was a subtle tension in her tone—almost as if she resented me for choosing a different direction. I, on the other hand, was in my element, excited to build my business and nowhere near ready to start a family. My company was my baby, and that seemed to irritate Emma.

"You're not getting any younger, Kim," she'd say, her tone carrying a hint of judgment. "Does starting a family not matter to you anymore?"

She knew it mattered to me—it would happen when the time was right—so her question didn't feel like genuine curiosity. It felt like judgment. Her snide jabs—"you're being selfish" . . . "you might live to regret this"—became impossible to ignore, running on repeat in my head. It was all I could talk about with John. Since no one in the world knew me better than my oldest friend, her opinions carried weight. I couldn't help but wonder: *Is she right? Am I chasing a dead-end dream? Maybe I should stop "being selfish" and start a family.*

Doubt had set in, and I hadn't realized the impact of the drip, drip, drip of criticisms, or how deeply I internalized them. The thing is, this wasn't just about Emma—she was reflecting the crushing weight of toxic societal norms that force women into impossible choices. Work or family, ambition or motherhood—always one at the expense of the other. The pressure to follow a timeline, to conform to roles that diminish individuality, leaves so many women feeling unseen and unworthy. I respected Emma's choices, but it didn't feel like she respected mine. Or maybe she resented them? Either way, I allowed it to take up far more space in my mind than it should have.

Of all the mistakes I'd made, this one took the longest to fully reveal its impact. Bad business deals announce themselves with red flags and alarm bells. Market downturns show up in numbers and charts. But toxic relationships? They masquerade as loyalty.

I learned this lesson not in a dramatic boardroom showdown or a failed pitch meeting but in my kitchen one night, when John finally broke our unspoken agreement to pretend everything was fine.

I was pouring my glass of red wine—my nightly ritual for "unwinding"—and was about to take it back to my office to keep working when John stopped me. "Kim, I don't recognize you anymore."

My first instinct was to be defensive. I was still me, just busier, more focused, more driven. Sure, I'd canceled our last few date nights, and maybe I wasn't sleeping great, and, yes, my office had basically become a bunker. But that's what building a successful company looks like, right?

"When was the last time you went to the gym, saw your friends, or ate a meal *not* at your desk? You're drinking every night, you barely smile, and you don't even notice how distant you've become," he said.

I stayed silent; I couldn't think of an answer to any of his questions. Suddenly, I went from feeling defensive to . . . exposed.

"You're mistaking self-destruction for hard work, and I can't watch it anymore. Something has to change," he added.

I poured my glass of wine into the sink and went back to my office. Sitting there, I realized he was right . . . about everything. I don't know if you've ever had an experience like that, but there's something truly terrifying about a person you love pointing out something so obvious you can't see.

How did I get here?

At that exact moment, my phone lit up with a text from Emma, as if the universe were answering the question for me.

Instead of texting back, I did what I always do in a crisis—I called my mom. No matter the situation, I can always count on her to tell me the unvarnished truth.

I poured it all out—Emma's nonstop criticisms, my doubts, my fears, everything John had said. The moment I vocalized everything, I realized my relationship with Emma had become toxic. I was only able to see the extent of the influence she was having on me once I zoomed out. My mom listened patiently, echoed John's concerns, and reminded me of a quote from entrepreneur Jim Rohn: "We are the average of the five people we spend the most time with."

I knew she was right. As moms usually are.

"And Kim," she said, knowing how much Emma's friendship had meant to me, "it's okay to grow apart from people. Sometimes, the healthiest thing you can do is let go, especially when a relationship is hurting, not helping you."

That day formed the foundation of one of my most deeply held beliefs: To achieve your greatest potential, it's imperative to be surrounded by people who support you, believe in you, and celebrate you. (I can hear my mom now, adding: "And that's true not just in business but life in general!")

The irony was that I was worried about hurting Emma's feelings when, for years, she didn't have any regard for mine. I reflected on my part in everything, too. Maybe I was too focused on my business, too consumed with my goals, and not attentive enough to our friendship. Unfortunately, none of it justified how negative Emma had become, and the conversation with my mom made me realize something:

The people who once lifted you up can also become the ones who hold you back.

It's important to point out that not every toxic situation is as straightforward as mine with Emma. Some people find themselves stuck in abusive or controlling relationships with no clear way to escape. I'm very aware that, for some people, leaving doesn't solely come down to courage—it can be a complex position where emotional, financial, and sometimes physical entanglement play a role. These situations require a different type of support to navigate. In my relationship with Emma, I had the privilege of deciding to leave on my own terms. And, as my mom reminded me, the choice to stay in this toxic relationship was not Emma's but my own.

I hadn't just held on to a toxic friendship; I had enabled it, becoming an accomplice to my own unhappiness. The real mistake was the hundreds of times I chose to excuse her toxic behavior. Each time I defended Emma, each time I rationalized her cutting remarks, I wasn't being loyal, I was betraying myself.

The twisted part was that I had made it all about me.

When she criticized my work ethic, I worked harder to prove her wrong.

When she questioned my life choices, I started second-guessing them.

When she diminished my successes, I began downplaying them, too.

I'd given her opinions so much power that I allowed them to dictate how I lived my life.

In the end, I chose to take a break from our friendship. That night I wrote her a heartfelt letter, expressing gratitude for our friendship but explaining that I had to distance myself in order to rebuild my confidence and self-esteem.

After sending it, I kept waiting for regret to set in, but it never did. Instead, I felt an overwhelming sense of . . . relief. I poured my energy into reconnecting with people who inspired me and believed in me without any trace of judgment. I reached out to mentors, made time for friendships I'd long neglected, and intentionally surrounded myself with positive people. By making this a priority, I felt a noticeable shift at work and at home. I noticed that I was no longer seeking validation from others, and I was learning to trust my instincts again. Slowly, my sense of self and confidence returned.

And guess what?

Emma never responded to my letter, and we haven't spoken since.

Relationships and friendships are living, breathing entities. They evolve, grow, and, sometimes, diminish. On her social media channels, relationship expert Esther Perel has pointed out a truth that many of us forget: Society doesn't prepare us for the end of friendships in the same way it does for romantic breakups.[15] As she says, friendship breakups can be just as heart-wrenching, if not more so. Yet even when a friendship turns toxic, we're expected to stay in the relationship no matter how harmful it becomes because "that's what friends do."

Over time, I've come to understand that letting go of Emma wasn't just about ending a toxic friendship; it was actually an act of self-love. I realized I was holding on to the memory of the supportive friend she used to be rather than the negative person she had become. Since then, surrounding myself with positive people has had the greatest impact on my success—an outcome that's supported by solid research.

One study examined the lives of self-made millionaires over a five-year period, and the findings demonstrated that associating with people who are positive and encouraging and work hard can foster those same qualities in you, too. Almost 180 millionaires were observed as part of the study—carried out by Thomas Corley for his book *Change Your Habits, Change Your Life*—and it was telling that they avoided people who had negative outlooks and blamed others for their own mistakes or circumstances.[16] The environments, communities, and networks we choose become important factors in determining our chances of success.

In the weeks that followed cutting the cord with Emma, I found myself examining all relationships in my life, both personal and professional. I wanted to take a good look at certain traits and patterns: Who were the people who lifted me up? Who drained my energy? Who would tell me the honest truth? Who had my best interest at heart? I have made it a priority to reflect regularly on all my relationships, to ensure that negativity doesn't seep into my inner circle again. I call this my "life audit." It's made a huge difference for me, and I am confident it could for you, too.

Here's how to perform your own life audit, step by step:

1. *Identify Your Inner Circle:* Write down the people you spend the most time with. Take a moment to reflect on those relationships.
2. *Evaluate Them Using the 3E Test:* Do they **energize, encourage,** and **elevate** you? If so, place a "+" next to their name.

3. *Assess Negative Influence:* Do they drain your energy or instill doubt? Are they overly critical? If so, put a "-" next to their name.
4. *Take Action:* Commit to dedicating more time and energy to the positive relationships, while setting boundaries to minimize or remove the negative influences.

After auditing out relationships that no longer serve me, I create the space to welcome new people and relationships. If, as the research shows, the people around us can have such a profound impact on our lives and success, shouldn't we be more intentional about cultivating more positive relationships?

The Four People Pillars

I knew I needed to curate my inner circle with the same care and attention that had proved foundational in building my business. That's when the concept of "people pillars" first came to me. In the same way a house requires strong pillars to be stable, we need pillars to support our growth and success. In that respect, we're the architects of our own empires. The strength and stability of what we build depend on the reliability and sturdiness of the pillars we put in place.

I grabbed a notebook and began sketching four pillars, considering what each one should represent. Those early scribblings now depict pillars that play a crucial role in supporting my life and career:

1. Pillar One: Experienced mentors
2. Pillar Two: Trusted friends and family
3. Pillar Three: All-star team members
4. Pillar Four: Like-minded peers

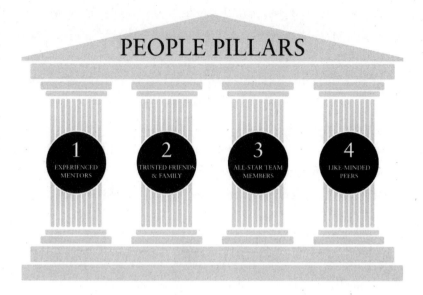

Incorporating this framework wasn't about avoiding toxic relationships; it was about proactively building a network of positive, supportive relationships that helped me grow. This single shift transformed my entire approach to life. As you read through each one below, consider which pillars currently stand strong in your life.

Pillar One: Experienced Mentors

Want to supercharge your success? Find a mentor.

Having mentors has made me 10 times more successful. And it's not just me. Some of the most successful people in the world have relied on a mentor to help them reach their goals. Bill Gates had Warren Buffett. Mark Zuckerberg had Steve Jobs. Oprah Winfrey had Maya Angelou. Luke Skywalker had Obi-Wan Kenobi! In fact, 93% of self-made millionaires have mentors.[17] And get this: People with mentors are promoted five times more than people without.[18]

It's impossible to overstate the value of having someone who can offer words of wisdom rooted in hard-earned experience when you're feeling stuck, overwhelmed, or even lost. Nine times out of ten, they will be familiar with the challenges you're facing and can help you to shift perspective or adopt a whole new approach.

Mentors don't always have to be in the same industry. Basketball legend Kobe Bryant once spoke about how Michael Jackson became an unexpected life-changing mentor.[19] Then 18, Kobe was working out at Gold's Gym in Venice Beach when the pop superstar called from his Neverland Ranch. That call led to a dinner where Jackson shared words of wisdom, reading material, and his support. Kobe soaked up all the guidance he could around mindset, mental approach, the pursuit of excellence, and daring to be different.

Like Kobe, I'm also lucky to have found a great mentor. While my mentor may not be the "King of Pop," he is the King of Branding. I got to know Chris Burch, co-founder of Tory Burch, in 2011 when I joined the board of a new internet startup. He was instrumental in guiding the company's branding and creative strategy with his 40 years of experience in building multiple companies with millions (and billions) in sales. At each board meeting, I made sure to absorb every nugget of wisdom he imparted. I had never met someone so brilliantly and innately creative. I also admired how open and transparent he was about his mistakes; he was happy to talk about what had gone wrong and why. His vulnerability was shocking and refreshing. Most leaders I knew masked all their insecurities and failures with bravado.

When I traveled to New York, we would meet at his favorite restaurant, Gramercy Tavern, and talk about our latest investments and business opportunities. We also got to know each other personally, and we quickly discovered we were both parents of twins (although his twins were 20 years older) and loved to travel. When it came to our life and business philosophy, we shared the same core values: kindness, generosity, and paying it forward. The more time we spent together, the more our friendship grew, and, even though we lived on opposite sides of the country, I made it a priority to connect with him often. Finding a mentor, and lifelong friend, as special as Chris has been one of the greatest gifts of my life.

Whenever I faced an obstacle around branding or marketing, he offered his wisdom and expertise. In many cases, I'm not sure I would have reached the answers or solutions as quickly without his input. That's the value of a mentor. You learn, grow, and improve because they have climbed the same mountains or overcome similar obstacles. To quote entrepreneur Jim Rohn again: "Seek out the mentors who will lead you to greatness in your field."

I've had many mentors at varying levels of success who have helped in different ways at different times; from my parents and grandparents, to teachers, coaches, bosses, and board members. If you don't have a mentor already, take proactive steps to find and develop those relationships.

A good mentor doesn't have to be a successful CEO or be 10 years further along the road than you are, but it does help if they're further along in terms of career, company, or project progress. Most importantly, though, your mentor should be invested in your success, keen to help you stay on track and hit your goals. Find a good mentor, and you will be deeply enriched by a relationship that grows over time. To help with your search, here are four steps to get started:

1. *Define Your Goals:* Write down what you hope to learn from a mentor. If you're starting a business, find someone with a proven track record. If you're stepping into a leadership role at a company, find someone who has been successful as a leader.

Be clear about what you're hoping to gain and the qualities/ guidance that will help you.

2. *Identify Potential Mentors:* Create a list of 5 to 10 people you admire, whether it's a leader/manager from the past or present, friends, coaches, or individuals in the community who have had a positive influence on you. It's usually easier if you have a direct relationship. But if you don't, it's often worth asking a mutual friend/associate to make an introduction. Simply identify an ideal mentor wish list.

3. *Request a Meeting:* Be bold, be confident, and ask for a 15- to 30-minute introductory call. Contact the potential mentor and be specific about the advice you need, and why they're the perfect person to provide it (it never hurts to compliment them!). The person you're reaching out to is probably busy, so be considerate about the amount of time you're asking for; it signals that you are respectful and grateful.

4. *Follow Up:* This is the crucial part. It's more than likely that the person you approached has numerous responsibilities and commitments. So if they don't respond initially, use the "triple tap" approach mentioned earlier in the book—send an email, follow up, and then, follow up again. If they still don't reply, move on without taking it personally. Sometimes, the timing isn't right. Remember, you want a mentor who has the time to give you.

With a mentor, treat it as a valued relationship. You might not be able to reciprocate with advice, but you can show appreciation for their wisdom. I can't begin to tell you what it means when a mentee takes the time to send a meaningful thank-you text or writes a thoughtful email expressing their gratitude. Treat all guidance as a gift with a value that will reveal itself over time.

Pillar Two: Trusted Friends and Family

There's a philosophy quiz I love, written by an unknown author, that invites us to reflect on the meaningful roles people play in our lives. It starts with these five prompts:

1. Name the five wealthiest people in the world.
2. Name the last five Heisman Trophy winners.
3. Name the last five winners of the Nobel Prize or Pulitzer Prize.
4. Name the last half dozen Academy Award winners for best actor or best actress.
5. Name the last decade's worth of World Series or Super Bowl winners.

I definitely couldn't answer any of these correctly, and I'm pretty sure the answers won't come easily to many people either. Now, answer these questions:

1. Name a teacher who aided your journey through school.
2. List three friends who have helped you through a difficult time.
3. Name five people who have taught you something worthwhile.
4. Think of a few people who have made you feel special.
5. Think of five people you enjoy spending time with.

I'll make a guess that the answers will come quickly to nearly everyone—and maybe even bring a few smiles. Because each of those memories have emotions and meaning attached. The people who make a difference in your life are not the ones with the most credentials, money, or awards, but the ones who care about YOU the most.

Typically, if we're going to find love, support, and guidance from anywhere, it's going to come from family or chosen family. You already know the people whose presence soothes you, whose advice you implicitly trust, and who have your best interests at heart. For me, it has always been my best friend, Sarajane; John; and my mom.

The loved ones you turn to don't need to be experts in your field of work; they simply need to be experts in helping you feel your best. Everyone experiences struggle and success. Everyone knows what it means to go through a tough time. What matters most is that your person is always there for you, listening without judgment and offering support. Can you think of someone who ticks all those boxes? If so, that's your pillar. Guard it with your life.

Pillar Three: All-Star Team Members

As you already know, my career didn't take off until I ditched the mistaken belief that I had to do everything on my own. Hiring a team enabled me to experience growth at a level I never thought possible.

As Dan Sullivan advises in his book *Who Not How*, stop asking "How can I do this?" and instead ask "Who can do this for me?" (I often reframe it as "Who can help me with this?")

A core team is so much more effective than any one individual can be, and scientific research has confirmed that fact since the 1980s.[20] Building a diverse, experienced team is invaluable for ideas, strategy, innovation, problem-solving, and support. The more you grow, the more you realize the value of all-star recruits.

If you aren't in the financial position to hire employees, think more creatively about who could be an adviser, consultant, partner, intern, or volunteer. You don't have to have employees to have a team. Whatever your vision, and whatever you're building, there are three specific areas I focus on when building an unstoppable team:

1. *Common Values:* These are the guiding principles that form the backbone of a company and its culture. Values serve as a compass for

making consistent decisions and to remind you of your North Star even in tough times. As Jim Collins writes in *Built to Last*, "Core values are the organization's essential and enduring tenets—a small set of general guiding principles; not to be confused with specific cultural or operational practices; not to be compromised for financial gain or short-term expediency."

When I started my first company, Frontline, my core values were passion, resilience, and opportunity. Passion because it represented an unwavering commitment, fueled by enthusiasm, purpose, and a genuine love for your work. Resilience because the industry around the internet was uncharted territory, so significant roadblocks were inevitable; we had to be comfortable with persevering despite setbacks. Opportunity because the individuals who worked for me not only sought out opportunities for themselves, but they also had a knack for recognizing opportunity where other people saw problems.

Together, these three values became "PRO." They guided my decisions, fostered team unity, and became the key traits I looked for in every hire over the next decade. Do you have a set of principles that shape your decisions, actions, and approach to life? If so, make them your core values. If not, start brainstorming values that have the most meaning. Select three or five and discuss them with your team to ensure the values resonate with everyone—the best values strengthen relationships and provide an endless source of pride and inspiration.

2. *Complementary Skills:* When building an all-star team, I focus on hiring people with skills that complement my own. I identify the areas that are my weak spots and the day-to-day tasks that I neglect the most. For example, while I understand the importance of accounting, I don't need to personally enter every transaction, so my first hire was a head of finance. I also had a vision for the technology needed to automate my business but lacked expertise in that area, so I hired

a vice president of technology with the necessary experience to bring my vision to life. In a startup environment, flexibility is crucial, so I look for people who aren't afraid to step outside their job title and take on whatever needs to be done. What are your strengths, and who do you need on your team to help you grow?

3. *Shared Goals and Celebrations:* Having a shared goal gives teams a clear target to shoot for and keeps everyone moving in the same direction. Nothing is more powerful than a team united in focus, mission, and direction, and it's important to recognize small wins to keep team morale high. Setting milestones on the way toward the bigger goal helps maintain momentum. After I established the goal of hitting $100 million in revenue at Frontline Direct, we celebrated the halfway milestone of $50 million by gifting everyone a pair of bright-blue Nike sneakers to keep them motivated as we sprinted toward the finish line. When we finally achieved the big 100, we threw a huge company party and gave everyone bonuses. Celebrating our success together reinforced a shared goal and strengthened team spirit. If you want to keep people motivated within a thriving culture, you need to make them feel valued.

Pillar Four: Like-Minded Peers

There's a dark side to entrepreneurship that nobody talks about at networking events or on social media: the 3 AM panic attacks, the forced smiles in meetings that downplay a crisis, and the crushing responsibility that sometimes feels overwhelming. It is all too easy to feel isolated as an entrepreneur, but isolation is not only unnecessary, it's downright dangerous to success. Experience has taught me that a peer group isn't only nice to have; in today's rapidly changing business landscape, it's a necessity. For me, there are three significant benefits:

1. Emotional Support: Being able to share my challenges with a group of trusted peers has helped me feel seen, supported, and understood in numerous situations over the years. Having like-minded people who understand what it means to be an entrepreneur has meant I've never felt alone; they provide me with a sense of belonging and emotional support—a priceless outlet for sharing, unloading, venting, and troubleshooting. Peer groups aren't just for entrepreneurs, either. Whatever support you're looking for—parenthood, health, content creation—there's a community waiting for you, via your inner circle, social media, Meetup.com, and community events. You can even start your own!

2. Network Connections: The ability to connect with other successful people can lead to new opportunities, partnerships, collaborations, and valuable insights, so the networking opportunities are endless. I've built friendships that have lasted over 20 years, and these are still the first people I turn to when I have questions or face challenges.

3. Accelerated Learning: The best shortcut to business success is learning from people who have made mistakes before you. That's why you're reading this book! However, you won't hear those invaluable stories unless you've established an inner circle of peers who feel comfortable sharing their failures and setbacks. In my peer group, we learned about what worked, what didn't, and what could have been done differently. Those are the kinds of golden insights we all need to help navigate the pitfalls and challenges ahead.

Your Inner Circle Defines Success

It's clear that the relationships we build—our people pillars—are the foundation of success, both personally and professionally. My experience with Emma taught me that when one of my core pillars turns toxic, it can impact my self-esteem, confidence, and ability to thrive. Leaving toxic relationships is not just about protecting your well-being, it's about reinforcing the pillars that support your future success.

I challenge you: Take a hard look at who's in your inner circle. View it as an extension of the life audit I mentioned earlier.

Do you have the right people helping you achieve your greatest potential?

Is your support structure sound and balanced, with each of your people pillars strong?

Are they pushing you to be better?

Are they exposing you to new ideas, opportunities, and people?

Do you leave conversations with them feeling energized?

If the answer to any of these questions is "no," it's time to take a step back and reflect.

Whether you need to find a mentor, spend more time with trusted friends and family, hire an all-star team, or join a peer group who will elevate you, now is the time to make your people pillars a priority. And as we close this chapter, I invite you to commit to finding those pillars in the next 30 days. Your future self will thank you for it. When you have the right people supporting you, you're not just prepared for success, you're primed for it.

LESSON IN THE MISTAKE

Toxic relationships limit your potential. The people in your inner circle don't just influence your mood—they shape your future.

CHAPTER SUMMARY

Self-reflection: Do you feel inspired, supported, and encouraged by the people around you? Whose energy lights you up and whose company drains you? Have you made excuses to keep negative relationships in life? Are you willing to let go of toxic relationships as an act of self-love?

Key Takeaways:

▶ **Your Inner Circle Defines Success:** Your success is directly tied to the people you spend the most time with. Take a hard look at who's in your inner circle. Are they pushing you to be better? Do they expose you to new ideas, opportunities, and people?

▶ **Let Go of Toxicity:** You decide whether to stay in a toxic relationship . . . or not. Letting go of toxic relationships is an act of self-love and respect. This makes space for new, positive relationships that align with the person you want to become.

▶ **Perform a "Life Audit":** Every year, conduct a life audit and take a good look at who are the positive influences in your life and who are the negative influences. Commit to dedicating more time and energy to the positive relationships in your life, while setting boundaries to minimize or remove the negative ones.

▶ **Build Your "People Pillars":** Develop a strong support network by curating the four people pillars in your life: *experienced mentors, trusted friends and family, all-star team members,* and *like-minded peers.* Each pillar creates a foundation for support and success.

▶ **Find a Mentor:** Seek out experienced mentors who can guide you through challenges and provide valuable insights. Successful people often credit mentors as a critical factor in their growth and success.

Millionaire Mindset: I choose to surround myself with people who uplift, inspire, and believe in me. I attract people who align with my vision and align with my values. I have the courage to let go of toxic relationships to make space for new positive ones. I deserve relationships that encourage my growth and celebrate my victories.

Staying Too Long

We often convince ourselves that staying is a sign of strength. But true strength lies in knowing when to let go. I wasted years refusing to leave my comfort zone. This mistake cost me the most valuable asset we have—time.

We've all been there: A dinner party goes late, the candles burn down, and the drinks are still flowing. While most people have said goodbye, a good number still linger. You glance at the time—10:56 PM—and think: *Am I staying too long?* If you're asking that question, the answer is nearly always yes! But you negotiate with yourself, through a sense of obligation, or fear of missing out, or politeness, and choose to stick around, not wanting to offend the host or come across as a downer. *I'll stay a little longer. Just one more drink.*

Cut to an hour later—people are still sipping wine and telling loud stories, and the host is dropping hints that it's time to wrap it up: switching off the music, turning up the lights, and talking about how tired he is.

The next morning, while feeling exhausted and nursing the worst hangover, you knew you should have left sooner! You followed the crowd, ignored your instincts, and paid the price of staying too long.

It's a scene from a dinner party, but it's also a common scenario in careers and relationships. Staying too long ranks as one of the biggest mistakes that can prevent people from achieving their goals and reaching their greatest potential. We know what we want to do but end up doing nothing. Why? Because the mind stirs up so much fear and doubt that we start making excuses that justify not taking action. *I'll give it a little longer. Just one more month.*

In relationships, people negotiate with themselves in a similar way. You can know that someone isn't right or that you've outgrown a significant other, but you persuade yourself to stay because the walls of a relationship feel safer than the unknown of being single again. And so people hold on to reasons to stay longer in the hope that things will improve.

Overall, it feels easier to stick with the familiar and the known. Fear, doubt, and a sense of obligation have the power to keep us stuck. People prefer safety over uncertainty, especially in their careers. One study found that 65% of Americans cling to the comfort of staying with their current employer.[21] Let's face it, most of us prefer comfort. And whether it's caused by a fear of the unknown, financial stability, or loyalty, we stay in stagnant situations too long.

I stayed in a job too long. And not just a few weeks or months. Years too long. Here's what happened.

When a company gets sold, the CEO doesn't just cash out and hit the beach. Instead, they're often bound by "golden handcuffs" in the form of an earnout agreement. This means that to make for a smooth transition, they're required to keep working to ensure that the acquirer gets what they paid for and, in exchange, they receive cash, stock, or other perks.

Normally, an earnout lasts anywhere from one to three years. Mine was three years when I sold Adconion to Amobee as part of the Singtel deal in 2014. I figured I'd transition out by early 2017 at the latest. Weeks turned to months. I kept telling myself I'd leave soon. Then 2018 came and went. Countless nights, I lay in bed thinking, *What am I doing?!* And then 2019 arrived. Honestly, at that point, I don't think I knew how to leave. I ended up staying almost *six years*.

Looking back, I can see that I stayed because of a narrative of obligation I had created: The company was "my baby," the employees my family, and we had all been invested in building the success that had led to the acquisition. Attachments from the past kept me in place, wrapped around a mistaken belief that I had a fiduciary and emotional duty to remain at the helm. What's more, our office in San Diego—where I lived at the time—was a grounding anchor. My happy place. My people. My memories. Why would I change anything? I know now that these were also my excuses, barely concealing the fear. The fear of letting people down. Fear of change. Fear of letting go. Fear of what I would do next.

Fear is the great equalizer. It doesn't care whether you've done a deal for $235 million or you're on a $55,000 salary.

"The team and company will be fine without you," John continually reminded me. Deep down, I knew that. I wasn't at my best working as an executive for a $40 billion telecommunication company in Singapore. Being an entrepreneur is core to my DNA, but I found comfort in the predictable routine when I should have been forward-thinking and chasing new opportunities. I rested on my laurels—a state of mind that risks turning into complacency.

That idiom "resting on your laurels" originated in the eighteenth century as a reflection of ancient Roman traditions where champion athletes and victorious military commanders were awarded laurel-wreath crowns in honor of their achievements. With such an accolade, and such status, these athletes and generals didn't need to achieve anything else to prove their talent, so they simply kicked back and basked in past glories.

I wasn't quite basking in glory, but I may have been guilty of basking in the comfort that glory had created. I had convinced myself that I was indispensable. I now laugh at the size of my ego back then, but, at the time, it felt real. I kept telling myself that the company will collapse without me . . . that my team needs me . . . that I can't abandon ship. I completely forgot the wisdom that my grandpa lived by.

Growing up, he always had a poem on his office wall called "The Indispensable Man" by Saxon White Kessinger—a humbling reminder that no matter how successful you are, you can always be replaced. A powerful metaphor within the poem illustrates this idea:

Take a bucket and fill it with water,
Put your hand in it up to the wrist,
Pull it out and the hole that's remaining
Is a measure of how much you'll be missed.

This simple imagery serves as a lesson in humility, reminding us that our absence leaves little lasting impact in the grand scheme of things.

As my grandpa always said after reciting that passage: "You might think you are indispensable. But I have learned that no one is."

I would soon learn that same lesson. Companies continue without us, no matter how much blood, sweat, and tears we pour in. If you're convincing yourself that you're indispensable, let the essence of this poem be a gentle reminder to you as well.

There is no such thing as job security. *It's an illusion.* Ask anyone who has had the dreaded 15-minute meeting suddenly appear on their calendar, only to show up and find their manager with an HR representative, reading a script to inform them, through a bunch of careful legalese, that their job is redundant. Or ask someone who thought they were going to a normal company meeting but instead walked blind into a mass layoff. Early on in my career, I thought I was "safe" as a top-performing employee, but my targets and sales figures counted for little when I was fired, too.

When there are bills and mortgages to pay, it's easy to cling to the illusion of security. Until that unexpected moment strikes, forcing us to confront the truth that we are, in fact, replaceable.

————

I had to confront my own truth in October 2019—the truth that I wasn't thriving in my role as CEO of Amobee. I had just welcomed my second set of twins and felt torn between being home with them and stepping back into my work responsibilities. It felt like an impossible choice and I struggled with it every day. After months of inner turmoil, I finally made the decision to leave. Or rather, the universe made it for me.

It was a gloomy afternoon in New York City, with rain pounding the cab windows as I inched through gridlocked traffic. My heart raced with every second that ticked by. I was already 40 minutes late for my flight to San Francisco, where I had an important board dinner. My mind raced, too. *Would I make it on time? Could I still get back by tomorrow night to help my older kids get ready for Halloween?*

Finally, the signs for JFK Airport rolled into view. Relief? Nope, not yet. As we headed down the airport entrance ramp, we hit . . . more traffic. The estimated time to reach the terminal jumped to 13 minutes, adding to my lateness with half a mile to go. Before even realizing it, I was out of the cab, on foot, running between cars, wheeling a suitcase in my three-inch heels. *I cannot miss this board dinner or Halloween with my kids!* The rain was relentless, transforming the road into a treacherously slick surface. And then, mid-sprint, disaster hit. My foot slipped and, in an instant, I was airborne, arms flailing, and I landed flat on my back with a jarring WHACK. I lay there dazed, staring up at planes taking off. The universe had hit me with a spiritual semitruck.

A man stretched his hand to help me up. "Are you okay?"

I was so embarrassed. I tried to stand but couldn't—my ankle had twisted. I hobbled into the airport, drenched and defeated, collapsed onto the nearest bench, and thought to myself, *What the hell am I doing?*

I knew at that moment what I needed to do. I called John and said, "I'm skipping the board dinner in San Francisco. I'm coming home."

Two months later, I officially announced that I was stepping down as CEO of Amobee to spend more time with my family and pursue my passion of supporting startup entrepreneurs. What the press release didn't say is that I also left to rediscover the passion I'd lost along the way.

The moment I broke free, I knew I should have done it much earlier.

I might not have known what the future held, but I didn't need to know. I trusted my intuition. I also trusted that something would present itself. That's the beauty of the unknown—it conceals opportunity until you step into its zone.

The timing ended up serving me well. It was early 2020, the pandemic was in full effect, and, like everyone else, I was stuck at home, feeling a strange mix of relief and utter exhaustion. Many people understandably want to forget how hard that time was, but, for me, it became a period of necessary and much-needed rest and reevaluation. As a new mom of twins, it gave me the opportunity to spend meaningful time with my family, reset, and step back to get clear on what I truly wanted to do next. It allowed me to think about the next chapter of my life in a way I hadn't before.

Cut to September 2020. With a renewed sense of freedom and energy, we embraced the unknown even more by moving from San Diego to Miami Beach. We swapped a community of friends and family for a city where we'd spent 10 days total and knew only one person. In a year when the global theme was overcautiousness, we threw caution to the wind. Some friends thought we were crazy. It was an election year, hurricane season, we had four kids under five years old, a seven-month-old English mastiff weighing 155 pounds, and we didn't have any family close by. On the surface, maybe those friends had a point.

But 2020 became our year of renewal, sparked by a sense of stagnation. Our new start would offer the opportunities I wanted to create, introduce me to new friends, and provide the warm, sunny lifestyle John and I loved. Miami was filled with energetic entrepreneurs and risk-takers who wanted to be moving, creating, and building. I found myself surrounded and embraced by a like-minded community where you could almost hear the entrepreneurial spirit fizzing in the air. On many evenings, John and I watched the sunset over the bay, and we shared the same thought: "What took us so long?"

The obvious answer to that question was me—I had stayed too long. But the moment I left Amobee and prioritized my own best interests—not the company's, not others', not nostalgia's—new opportunities opened up in unexpected ways. A powerful reminder of the magic that comes with embracing change and stepping into the life you're meant to live.

The Five Traps That Hold Us Back

Over the years, I've seen friends and colleagues stay too long in jobs, relationships, and unproductive situations. I call it "a state of stagnation" because it keeps us stuck and going nowhere, rather than moving forward and growing. Of course, walking away from something meaningful is easier said than done. The layers of complexity are different for everyone, even if the reasons that we hold on are often the same. You can know it's time to leave, yet the mere thought of "starting over" feels daunting. But no one builds massive success by staying comfortable and avoiding tough decisions. There's no signpost that says "Easy Route—This Way." Successful people actively embrace risk, befriend discomfort, and continuously push past their own limits.

What I've observed in varied circumstances, including my own, are the five common traps of our human nature that tend to hold people back. Which is why it's essential to understand how they keep us stuck and how to break free from them. The traps that follow can be equally applied to friendships, marriage, clients, business ventures, places, or anything else into which you've invested time, energy, and emotion.

1. The Financial Stability Trap

The allure of financial security is an enticing trap. We fear losing the stability of a regular paycheck, the benefits, and the ability to meet our car or mortgage payment, making it hard to walk away from what feels safe. As Kevin O'Leary from *Shark Tank* says, "A salary is a drug they give you to make you forget about your dreams."

Let me tell you about Sarah, a woman I recently started mentoring. She is a talented marketing director who has worked for the same company for six years. The first time we met for coffee, she shared how she hadn't been promoted or received a raise in two years. When I asked why she stayed, she gave me that all-too-familiar response: "It's stable, you know? I've got bills to pay, a mortgage to cover, and the health insurance is good. I can't risk losing that security. I'm sure they'll give me a raise soon."

I knew it was time to get real with her. "Sarah, the truth is you think you're playing it safe, but, by staying, you're actually leaving money on the table."

I could tell that she didn't understand what I meant. So I explained how, on average, people who stay in the same job receive a year-over-year salary increase of 5%, whereas people who change jobs see salaries increase by 9.7%.[22] What's more, 60% of people who leave their jobs end up seeing an increase in their real earnings at their new company.[23]

These findings underscore the point that it costs *more* to stay in a job—you are earning less and stunting your career growth. In some cases, I've seen people earning above the market rate, but, more often than not, most are underpaid relative to market value or industry standards.

This data was the reality check Sarah needed. She'd been so focused on a stable paycheck that she completely missed out on the financial growth that comes with a new opportunity. I encouraged her to research what her peers were earning at competing companies and to consider if she was getting paid what she was worth. That one nudge was all it took to set Sarah free from her limited thinking.

Two months later, she emailed me to say she'd finally taken the leap and landed a new job. Her salary? A significant 30% more than what she had been earning.

The takeaway is clear: Sometimes the biggest risk is not taking any risk at all. Your financial stability isn't just about holding on to what you have—it's about continually exploring how to grow your career to position yourself for greater success. Whatever job you have, you should always be learning or earning. If you are not doing either, it's time to make a change.

How many times have you known someone who stayed too long in a job, without getting a raise or promoted, leaving them feeling unrecognized and underappreciated? They stick around, while a colleague who leaves after just two years lands a significant pay jump elsewhere. If you're someone who's staying for reasons of financial stability, you need to figure out whether that's an excuse or if you're genuinely happy where you are.

To determine if you're caught in the financial security trap, ask yourself these five questions:

1. Have you had a meaningful promotion in the past two years?
2. Have you gotten a raise of more than 5% in that same period?
3. Are you learning new skills?
4. Are you happy and fulfilled with your work?
5. Are you sacrificing personal growth for financial comfort?

If you answered "no" to most of those questions, it's time to make it a priority to find a new opportunity. A two-to-three-year window is the ideal time frame to stay somewhere without getting a raise or promotion—to learn, contribute, and master a role before looking to advance to the next level. If there is no more room for you to grow your skills at your current company, then where is the value in staying? It's also important to consider the message you might be sending by staying too long. You may think it suggests consistency, dependability, and dedication but, to a future hiring manager, it could just as likely suggest apathy or a lack of ambition. Of course, there are rare exceptions when staying at one company for too long actually pays off.

Take Nike CEO Elliott Hill, who was appointed as chief executive and president in October 2024. He started in 1988 and never left. Then, aged 60, he landed the top job. Looking at his resume, it's clear Elliott refused to stand still. From 1988 to 2024, he didn't stay in one role for longer than three years. (Read that again. *He didn't stay for longer than three years in a role.*) He found a job he loved, people he loved working with, a workplace where he could thrive, and he kept challenging himself . . . and growing.

You can't know what's possible until you take a chance on your-self; and by taking a chance on yourself, you invite the prospect of surprising yourself.

Have the courage to be your own career advocate—to keep open-ing the door to better compensation and career growth. The cost of staying could well outweigh the cost of leaving, and you owe it to yourself to find out.

2. "Fear of the Unknown" Trap

Humans are creatures of comfort. We don't do well with uncertainty. It's why fear of the unknown is so common. We prefer guarantees.

But there's only one guarantee in life—change. It's the one con-stant, an unstoppable force that forever shapes and impacts our lives. *Nothing* stays the same. Our bodies age. Relationships transform. Environments evolve. Technology advances. Everything around us is always changing. Maybe that's why we run from uncertainty and instead try to hold on to what's familiar and comfortable. None of us are the same person we once were, so why try to live the same life? And that's the trap—fearing the unknown to such a degree that you don't invite change.

Change is scary. But regret is way, way scarier. And personally, I'd rather face an ocean of change than a mountain of regret. Uncertainty is opportunity in disguise. We just have to remove the cloak of fear and see the beauty underneath. Don't view the unknown as a nega-tive. Embrace it as a positive. A new beginning. A fresh adventure. A plot twist in your story.

My friend Mary was four years into a well-paid role in healthcare when she told me she was afraid to leave because she didn't know what would happen if she did. For 18 months, she'd felt undervalued, underappreciated, and desperate to leave. "But what if the alternative is not better than where I'm at now?" she asked. If Mary were still single without two children, she would have trusted the unknown far more, she said. But the stakes were higher now that she had a family; the risk was much greater. Understandably, that's what made Mary hesitant to jump, and so her dream to launch a consultancy business waited in the wings.

"What if it all goes wrong?" she said.

"What if it all goes right?" I said.

That made her think. Too many people spend so much time contemplating negative outcomes, but what about the other side of the coin? All you have to do is flip the switch and consider positive outcomes instead. That's why I gave Mary an exercise that can help anyone break free from the limitations of fear.

Think back to a time when you experienced a big change in life—whether voluntary or beyond your control—and recognize how you have previously navigated the unknown. Whatever the circumstances, you will have started from a place of uncertainty. It may well have been stressful or scary, but you adapted and kept moving forward. Ask yourself: What did I learn? How did it make me better? What opportunities emerged? What successes happened because of the actions I took?

Mary decided to stay at her job a little longer while launching a brand and marketing business as a side hustle. She set a clear goal: Once the income from her consultancy reached 80% of her salary, she would leave her job and go all in. Sure enough, six months later, as more and more clients came in, she hit her goal and left her job.

More often than not, we can look back and realize that periods of uncertainty led to great turning points or moments of transformation in our lives. It's a reminder that there are *benefits* to change; that we can choose to be energized by uncertainty, not intimidated by it. As I often say, the unknown is only unknown until you make it known!

3. The Loyalty Trap

Loyalty is an admirable quality. I'd argue that it's one of the most valued traits in the workplace, because it builds trust, cements solidarity, and spreads a sense of collective pride. Without its binding effect, a company cannot foster a thriving culture. However, loyalty crosses into unhealthy territory when it turns into blind devotion. This is where people risk falling into the loyalty trap.

That trap is set when loyalty to a company or boss begins to eclipse loyalty to yourself, placing your own interests on the back burner. Corporate America plays its part in making this trap feel unnoticeable by cultivating the psychological ties that keep employees believing there is value and longevity in loyalty. You hear it all the time in the workplace. "We're a team!" or "We're a family!" or "We're all in this together!" But when challenging times come and the waters get rough, who are the first to be let go? Talk of team, family, and togetherness often feels hollow, revealing that the foundations of our sense of stability aren't as solid as we'd like to believe.

Of course, if you're a Navy SEAL or a US Army soldier, your interests will always come second to a sense of duty and the oath of allegiance. But generally speaking, it's a trap.

I've been in business a long time, so I've heard a lot of excuses about why people choose to stay, even when they're unhappy. The most common excuse is emotional attachment: to colleagues, to a place, to a mission. I know how hard this can be. I was trapped in the same predicament, feeling obligated to stay for my team because they felt like family. But loyalty is not loyalty *if* it compromises your growth—that's the trap. This universal struggle is perfectly personi-fied through my friend Michelle, whom I've known for 15 years.

She's a real estate assistant, and, based on her Instagram, you'd think she loves selling houses more than anything. But, as her friend, I know that those perfectly edited photos don't match reality. For years, she dreamed of opening her own clothing boutique. She'd excel at it, too. The Michelle I know comes alive when talking about vin-tage clothes and fashion trends, not floor plans and mortgage rates.

She hadn't left her real estate firm for one reason: loyalty to a boss who she believed couldn't function without her. This boss relied on her for *everything*: scheduling, marketing, open houses, and even writing emails.

Over dinner one night, Michelle told me she wanted to quit but felt like the whole operation would crumble without her. "I don't know how my boss would cope," she said. "Plus, she'd feel betrayed and abandoned."

"How *she* would cope and feel is not your problem, Michelle," I pointed out. "Your focus needs to be on your own growth and happiness."

On an intellectual level, Michelle understood this, but on an emotional level, she cared (almost too much) about her boss's feelings. "I don't know if I can bring myself to do it."

This is the loyalty trap in action. Or I should say, the misguided loyalty trap. And Michelle was so trapped that she put her dreams in the back seat. I reminded her that the company wouldn't fold without her, and that her time to follow her dream was *now*!

"You owe this to yourself," I told her.

I wasn't saying anything that Michelle didn't know already, but she needed a nudge to make the leap. A month later, she handed in her notice and, even though the boss tried to guilt her into staying, she held firm in her newfound loyalty to herself. She's now moving forward with her dreams to launch a boutique and couldn't be happier.

When you lose sight of your own best interests, it's time to step back and reevaluate your priorities, because loyalty has clouded your judgment. Is the loyalty reciprocated? Are you being recognized and rewarded? If the answer to either of those questions is "no," you need to examine whether you're trapped by misguided loyalty. If being a success and making money is the goal, staying true, and loyal, to yourself must be your top priority.

4. The Identity Trap

Who are you without your job? Strip away the title, the role, and the professional persona, and what are you left with? The answer is you, with all your unique strengths and talents, your friends and family, and your hobbies and passions. Basically, you're left with everything that makes you who you are *outside of work*.

Too often, people lose themselves in what they do, which leads to overly identifying with a job or role that ultimately keeps them trapped. Usually, people only come to realize how much their identity has become intertwined with their job once they've left. They've derived so much pride, worth, status, and purpose from what they do that they suddenly feel lost without it all.

How many times have you seen someone go through an identity crisis when laid off or struggling with retirement? It usually means they've poured 100% of themselves into the company, sacrificing their own sense of self. I know this firsthand. It's the reason why I didn't move on from Amobee sooner. I didn't know how to separate my true self from *my* identity as a tech CEO. That's what had defined me for 20 years, and I felt deeply connected to that role and way of life—to the extent that I struggled to imagine doing anything else. I would eventually come to understand that "Tech CEO" was just the label, and it didn't need to define me, in the same way the clothes I wear and the car I drive don't define me. Recognizing and redefining our sense of self—beyond job titles, beyond what we do for a living—is key to breaking free from the identity trap.

My friend Nina had to learn this same lesson when she was laid off from her senior role with a luxury fashion label. "Whenever I introduced myself to someone, I said my name, followed by the brand," she said. "It gave me immediate street cred. People instantly took me seriously."

Losing that job felt like losing a piece of herself. "That's the one thing I struggled with the most," she said. "The identity I had built at work made my sense of self feel anchored, even when I loathed the job."

Only when forced to walk away did she come to understand that no amount of prestige is worth the misery. "I wasn't even happy and yet I hung on to this identity . . . for the status," she said.

Today, Nina is a fashion stylist, feels liberated, and answers to no one but herself. "I should've done this years ago!" she told me. Who you are isn't solely defined by what you do. So if you feel your identity is too closely tied to your work, ask yourself these two simple questions: What matters most to me beyond my work? Is what I'm doing fulfilling me and making me happy?

It's one thing being genuinely proud of your work or company, but it veers into unhealthy territory when your sense of worth is attached to pay, power, or, as in Nina's case, prestige. That normally means you've lost yourself somewhere along the way. Moving on can become even harder then, because, in your own mind, you're leaving behind a part of yourself.

If you feel your personal-professional identity has merged in this way, it's time to get back to yourself. Prioritize "me time" or time with friends and family. Engage in more activities outside of work. Start doing more for yourself—something that fills *your* cup. Set personal goals around health, hobbies, or travel. By dedicating more time to your life *outside of work,* you will build a more holistic identity and become balanced with your values, passions, and what brings you joy. You become defined by the life you lead, not the job you do.

5. The Comfort-Zone Trap

Let me introduce you to my friend Ted, who perfectly illustrates what it means to be caught in the comfort-zone trap. Ted has always been passionate about fitness. He runs marathons and does cold plunges at 5 AM. His wife jokes that his best friend is his mountain bike. Since I've known him, he has had this "crazy" dream of one day starting his own gym. But to me, it doesn't sound so crazy. Whenever he talks about it, he's a whole different Ted—animated, optimistic, and passionate. It's in stark contrast with how he talks about his actual job as a software sales executive where he's unengaged and uninspired. He's been at the same company for seven years, and he's far too comfortable. And being comfortable has kept him from chasing the thing that truly excites him. That's exactly what the comfort-zone trap looks like—playing it safe instead of pushing toward something greater.

Recently, he and I were catching up while our kids played in the pool, and he shared his dilemma. "There's only one thing stopping me from leaving—time, money, and courage."

He was half joking, but I asked: "Are you happy?"

"I'm happy that I can put a roof over my family's head," he said.

I've encountered countless Teds over the years, caught between comfort and ambition. While they seem content, there's often a spark missing or lack of passion for what they do. But the mere idea of detaching from everything that's stable keeps them rooted in the same place.

If there's a common denominator running through all the stories I've shared, it's the comfort zone. It is the psychological state of predictability, usually in an environment where you feel in control. To move beyond this state would involve risk and a change of habit. It would invite uncertainty and fear and all the accompanying anxiety.

Scientists and human behaviorists have long been fascinated by the limitations we impose on ourselves, ever since two Harvard psychologists first studied the idea of a comfort zone in 1908.[24] Robert M. Yerkes and John Dillingham Dodson found that if our stress levels are too low, we can't perform at our best; on the flip side, if stress levels are too high, our performance deteriorates. So it's all about finding that sweet spot in between, which exists *outside* of the comfort zone but doesn't take us to the extreme edges of the unknown.

For me, it boils down to one of the most meaningful questions: What do you want out of life? If you're reading this book, I'm guessing you're looking to level up—maybe to earn more money or to chase a passion where purpose matters more than a paycheck. Either way, none of it is going to happen if you stick with what's comfortable.

Pursuing a dream, a vision, or a purpose that lights you up is always going to involve an element of risk. I've yet to meet a successful individual—in business, in sports, in life—who didn't invite risk at the same time as inviting opportunity. They tend to go hand in hand.

Whenever I talk with someone who admits they're stuck in the comfort zone, I ask, "Are you truly content, or do you think this is as good as it gets?"

I ask that question because, when people *really* start to open up, they always say something about wanting *more* from life—bigger dreams, new achievements, different experiences. But the self-imposed comfort zone has become a barrier blocking progress. So the ultimate self-reflection to sit with boils down to this: "Am I truly comfortable? Or am I just settling?"

If you're unsure, here are some common signs to help you know if it's time to shake things up. It's when you're:

Comfortable but restless

Stagnating, not learning or growing

Constantly tired or emotionally drained

Feeling undervalued, underappreciated, or taken for granted

Searching for a greater purpose to feel more fulfilled

These are indicators that you've outgrown where you are. But even if you decide it's time to move on, you still have to make it happen. Pure intent alone doesn't make it any easier to trigger change. Think how hard it can be to simply hit the gym and maintain a new fitness routine. When you are in the habit of something—a job, a relationship, a routine of any kind—it's challenging to switch things up.

I knew that I needed to leave my company, but, out of loyalty to my team, I extended my stay in the comfort zone because it felt safe and familiar. Take a moment to consider this question: What dreams would you pursue if you knew that on the other side of your hesitation, incredible growth and transformation awaited?

If you truly want to change your life for the better, you must be willing to be uncomfortable. If you're not feeling at least some discomfort while chasing your dreams, it's a sign you're playing it too safe.

Maybe you know what you *should* do, but what do you *want* to do?

Deep down, you know what you can no longer tolerate and what vision, idea, or dream ignites your energy. So why stay somewhere that doesn't align with your future? Believe in yourself, make a plan, push forward, and forge a new path. Remember, no one ever made millions by standing still.

The "Exit Ramp" Strategy

It can be scary to even think about leaving a job, a relationship, or a community. But the more mentally prepared you are, the easier it becomes. That's where the "exit ramp" strategy comes in—a thought-ful approach that helps you chart your path forward. It's about mapping the way ahead, knowing where the off-ramp is, and creating a practical plan for what comes next.

If you're looking to move jobs, research the job market and explore all options.

If you're looking to go freelance, build your resources and start networking.

If you're looking to pursue a dream, start working on it in your spare time.

If you're looking to launch a startup, do market research and write up a business plan.

"But I don't have any spare time!" is what a lot of people tell me when I say that. A little gentle prodding soon uncovers the fact that they do have plenty of time—they're just not managing or prioritizing it. "An eight-hour workday is a half day," my dad always said. "If that's all you're putting in, you're going to be like everyone else."

Here's how I see it: You've got 24 hours in a day. Eight hours to earn your salary. Eight hours to sleep. And eight hours to do whatever you like. Some people use that bonus time for leisure, some for rest, but you could utilize that precious time to your advantage—to build, to network, to create.

In today's busy world, a lot of people feel overscheduled and over-worked, and you might feel the need to simply unwind, recharge, and connect with family. So, yes, carve out time and space for the import-ant things. But you can also be smart about maximizing whatever extra hours you have and channel those hours into your business idea, or side hustle, or whatever dream consumes your waking thoughts.

Brian Armstrong built the Coinbase crypto app by going "hard at it" in his spare time, maximizing his nights and weekends while hold-ing down a full-time day job at Airbnb where his days didn't finish until 7 PM. "I'd come home, eat dinner, and then work from eight PM to midnight," he told the *Startup Archive* podcast. "I would do that maybe three to four days on weekdays. And then, on the weekend, I'd work Sundays for seven or eight hours." He maintained that schedule for 18 months, using "my determination to build something important as my fuel."

Brian dedicated four hours a night, and most of his Sundays, to his passion, and that dedication was well invested. He co-founded Coinbase in 2012, and it is now one of the largest crypto exchanges in the world, with seven million monthly users and, by the end of 2024, a valuation of $8 billion.

What time can you set aside to pursue your passion? Maybe you can get up an hour earlier every day. Maybe you can find two hours a night three times a week. Great! Any bonus time you can dedicate to your vision is time well invested.

If you're in a marriage or relationship, include your partner in your game plan, explaining your strategy. When I shared with John why I was working so hard during those early years in Hawaii, he understood that I was working to build a better future for us. He only understood that because I communicated my reasoning clearly—we were making a short-term sacrifice to create the life we envisioned long-term.

I squeezed every last second out of every waking hour while working from that kitchen table, building and growing my first business. Working 16- to 18-hour days didn't leave room for much of a social life and didn't initially make me much money either. But the payoff to those early sacrifices turned out to be the lifestyle and freedom I enjoy today. It's the "beans now, steak later" approach that Kevin O'Leary wrote about in his book *Cold Hard Truth on Men, Women & Money*.

Success demands that we make sacrifices long before it delivers the rewards.

So, how badly do you want to succeed? Every coach asks an athlete the same question. It's the relentless pursuit of excellence that sets apart the winners. Kobe Bryant's famous training ethic was built on the knowledge that there is always someone prepared to work harder . . . and that's what pushed him the extra mile. He stayed longer in the gym, practiced an extra hour on the court, and made 400 more shots than other players. Focus. Dedication. Precision. Sacrifice. The hallmarks of a champion.

The discipline you bring to your own life will determine your level of success. Those extra eight hours are there to be maximized or wasted. So what can you do today to start preparing the groundwork for the future? Here are three exercises to help you prepare:

Code Your Confidence: Unlocking confidence unlocks doors to opportunity. People hear your confidence in how you communicate, they see it in how you hold yourself, and they feel it in your interactions and decision-making. A lack of confidence can hold you back, so start building it now and, over time, it will develop. Write down a list of your strengths, skills, accomplishments, and what makes you unique. View this list as a highlight reel to combat self-doubt or fear. But be sure to ask three of your closest friends what they think your top strengths are, too, because we can sometimes underestimate or overlook certain talents. Take those positive observations and use them as your confidence armor. I've often said confidence is a practice—the more you wear it and speak it, the more confident you will be.

Think Big, Start Small: Successful people dream big and take action. Consider what small, practical steps you can take to get the ball rolling. Update your resume. Research job opportunities. Create a business plan. Write out a list of goals. Apply for a new position. Get into the habit of focusing on your future by building a habit of taking small, proactive steps. If leaving your job feels scary, this is a good way to move gradually toward a bigger goal.

Invest in Yourself: What are you doing to invest in *you*? That's where your time, focus, and energy need to be channeled. It's the first piece of advice I give anyone looking to level up. Invest in learning by taking a course or reading a new book. Invest in growing by finding a mentor. Invest in your physical and mental well-being by meditating, going to the gym, or eating healthy. Prioritize investing in yourself and watch how it pays off.

With each of these exercises, you're training the mind to step away from what's familiar. If you feel any fear or discomfort, know that it's only happening because you are stretching yourself (or at least thinking about it). That's a good thing! If I don't feel regularly challenged by my work—if it's not pushing me to improve—then I know it's time for a change.

One-Year Success Plan

It might take three months. It might take six. It could even take a year. Change takes time, even if you've done all the groundwork. Being mentally prepared and getting everything lined up is a start; it's another matter to actually execute the plan and take the leap.

That's why I always suggest creating a "one-year success plan."

You could be leaving a company, launching a business in the months after quitting, or embarking on a new creative project, but, whatever the case, as the well-known saying goes, "If you fail to plan, you are planning to fail."

So first *capture your vision.* Where do you want to be one year from now? What do you want to accomplish? Who do you want to become? Answering those three questions will create a mini mission statement. For example: "I want to go to Los Angeles, launch and build a tech startup, and be known as a successful CEO." Keep that statement front and center—pin it to your laptop, desk, or bathroom mirror—as a reminder that keeps you on track.

Then *start working backward*. Build a framework of milestones you need to hit. Use a spreadsheet, a blank page, or a calendar. What's the second-to-last thing you need to do before leaping? And before that? This reverse-engineering process will help you get a sense of what you need to accomplish and how long each step will take.

Next, *do the hardest thing first*. That could involve having a hard conversation or conducting some market research. Basically, it's any task that feels daunting to start or complete but is important to getting your idea off the ground.

Finally, *find an accountability partner*. Make sure you choose someone who's reliable and strong enough to keep you on track, and that means someone capable of asking the hard questions and keeping you honest.

To set yourself up for success, provide yourself the runway of a year. You might be ready in half that time, but at least you have mapped out the way ahead and set a deadline. That year will allow you to test ideas, backtrack, revise, and keep iterating. If you need help with this plan, I've created a free "One-Year Success Plan" template with a step-by-step, month-by-month plan. You can access it at www .KimPerell.com/Resources.

Breaking Free

Having read this far, you already know the price of staying too long. At this point, the question is: Are you ready to break free from the fears, doubts, and excuses? Are you ready to bet on yourself?

When I finally stepped away from my last company, Amobee, I reignited a passion I didn't even realize I had lost. Leaving eventually led to more success than I could ever have imagined. Change is never easy, but it's where true growth begins. If you want things to get better, only YOU have the power to make it happen. Yes, finding a new job requires effort. Yes, it can be daunting and exhausting. But there's no comfort in the growth zone, and there's no growth in the comfort zone. What do you value most? If you want to be a success and make that first million, you have to leave the safe harbor and set sail for new horizons.

So here's my challenge to you: Be brave. Take the leap. Don't settle for a life that's just okay when an extraordinary one is waiting just beyond the horizon. Remember, whether you are leaving a job, starting a business, or making a bold change, you were not born to play small. Trust in your journey, trust in your instincts, and step into your full potential.

LESSON IN THE MISTAKE

Staying too long is a choice,
and so is leaving. The
universe doesn't open new
doors until you have the
courage to close the old ones.

CHAPTER SUMMARY

Self-reflection: Have you stayed in a job or relationship too long? What is preventing you from making a change?

Key Takeaways:

▶ **No One Is Indispensable:** Job security is an illusion—a belief we hold on to for our own comfort. Make sure you are learning new skills, investing in new relationships, and seeking out new opportunities.

▶ **You May Earn Less by Staying:** Research shows that people who switched jobs saw their salaries increase by 9.7%, compared with people who stayed in the same job and received an increase of 5%. You should always be learning or earning!

▶ **The Five Traps That Keep You Stuck:** A state of stagnation leaves us stuck when we feel trapped by finances, fear of the unknown, the comfort zone, and matters of loyalty and identity. Which of these traps may be holding you back from making a change?

▶ **Know Your "Exit Ramp" Strategy:** Have a game plan for the day when you decide to leave. Do your research. Build your resources. Plan ahead.

▶ **The One-Year Success Plan:** To set you up for success, give yourself a year's runway. Capture your vision. Know what you need to do. Find an accountability partner. Set a deadline. Download your personal success plan at www.KimPerell.com/Resources.

Millionaire Mindset: I embrace change, trusting that moving forward is better than standing still. Letting go of fear, I visualize what can go right, not what can go wrong. I step into the unknown and allow life to unfold.

Failing to Pivot

Businesses don't fail because the world changes.
Businesses fail because they don't adapt. I thought
sticking to a plan showed commitment. The truth is,
I was stubborn . . . and paid the price for it.

The year was 2006. The internet was still in its awkward teenage years, and digital advertising was the Wild West. I was a relentlessly ambitious entrepreneur with a recently launched digital marketing company. As the new cowgirl in town, I had two services in my holster: search engine optimization (SEO) and email marketing. Business was booming, and I felt on top of the world. But then, like a distant rumble of thunder, I heard murmurs about something called "social media." I brushed it off for a year. How big could this trendy "social media thing" get, right?

Soon enough, those murmurs turned into a roar as Facebook exploded onto the scene. Meanwhile, there I was, still selling SEO and email marketing like it was 1999. And then, my outdated ways lost me a client—my biggest client.

I'll never forget that day. I breezed in for what I thought would be a routine quarterly meeting. Instead, I walked into a conference room of grim faces. My client said, "Kim, we need a partner who can handle our social media marketing needs. We're sorry, but we're moving our business to someone with that expertise."

I paid the price for not embracing emerging new trends. I had allowed myself to become outdated. Not by ignorance, not by bad luck, but by a conscious decision to cling to what felt familiar and comfortable. My stubbornness wasn't just about being set in my ways—it was about ego. I had convinced myself that my early success meant I knew better than everyone else. When clients would mention Facebook, I dismissed them with an overconfident speech about "tried and true methods." I was the "digital expert," after all. For someone who prided themself on being an early adopter, I had never been more blind. It wasn't just a mistake. It was arrogance disguised as expertise, and I paid for it. How did it feel? Humiliating.

That night, I sat in my office until 2 AM, switching between staring at the wall and staring at a spreadsheet that showed our growth stagnating. The weight of my mistake pressed down on me. I felt small, unprepared, and worst of all, exposed. The very qualities that had once made me successful—my focus, my drive, my unyielding commitment to the plan—were the same qualities that blinded me. I was stuck in a time capsule of my own making, and the world outside was moving on without me.

Every time someone asked me about social media, I brushed it off. "It will never be that big for advertisers," I'd say confidently—making two mistakes at once: ignoring a client's need and not paying attention to emerging trends.

That's the thing about mistakes like this: They force you to face the reality that you are not invincible. I'd always prided myself on being ahead of the curve, but in that moment, I realized I'd become something I never wanted to be—out of touch. It wasn't just the loss of the client that stung; it was also the deeper realization that I'd let my ego steer the ship. I had ignored the whispers of change, and by the time they became loud enough, the damage was done.

At that moment, the choice was undeniable for my business: pivot or perish.

Whether it's the high-stakes world of entrepreneurship or a situation where something feels stagnant, there's only one skill that separates the survivors from the casualties: the ability to pivot. It's not just a buzzword; it's the lifeline that can pull you back from the brink of failure and catapult you into unexpected success.

The next morning, I knew exactly what needed to happen. I called an emergency team meeting. "We're going all in on social media," I told them. The surprised looks on their faces told me this was going to be a dramatic pivot, but I reminded them that one of our core values was *opportunity*.

"I was wrong," I admitted, my voice heavy with the weight of realization. "We need to pivot. Think of it as a course correction. There's the plan we originally had, and then there's the reality we're facing now. Our current strategy isn't delivering the growth we envision, and I take responsibility for that. But what matters most is what we do next, so it's time to rethink, reorganize, and react."

I developed "the three *R*'s" as a decision-making framework to help quickly assess what a potential pivot would look like.

Rethink: Step back and analyze the situation without bias toward the original plan.

Reorganize: Decide the best course of action and reorganize resources accordingly.

React: Implement the decision in a timely manner.

In business, timely action is critical—delaying decisions can lead to greater setbacks. The ability to respond swiftly and decisively can make the difference between overcoming obstacles and being left behind.

There is no shame in admitting the need to take a different direction. It doesn't always mean you've made a mistake; it often means that something about the landscape has shifted. A pivot is a *response* to market dynamics or consumer behavior. Once I emphasized that to my team, they jumped on board, understanding the urgency of learning a new skill and overhauling our strategy.

That one decision supercharged our success.

As we leaned in to social media, a wave of relief washed over me, bringing with it a newfound energy. I felt an overwhelming sense of gratitude that we had the courage to confront our missteps before they turned into missed opportunities. It wasn't easy, but it proved to be the turning point we desperately needed.

As the digital landscape continued to evolve, so did we. It became my mission to be the first to adopt new digital marketing channels as they emerged—Instagram, Snapchat, LinkedIn, out-of-home advertising (digital billboards), connected TV (placing ads alongside streaming shows), and podcasts. Over the next decade, our social media business skyrocketed, hitting an incredible $200 million in annual revenue!

Many of the greatest companies in the world made fundamental pivots that transformed their businesses. Consider how these giants started out:

- YouTube launched as a video-dating site.
- Amazon was only an online bookstore.
- Twitter first set out to provide accessibility to podcasts.
- Netflix began with mail-order DVDs in the US only.
- Starbucks only sold coffee beans.

They all took a chance, made a bold move, and the rest is history. The list goes on and on. Most businesses that thrive have had to pivot at one point or another. It's the reality of the business world—nothing is guaranteed, and the path to success is almost never a straight line.

The need to course correct can happen for numerous reasons—market forces, misjudgments, shifts in culture, developments in technology, or recognizing an unmissable opportunity. The skill lies in identifying those moments and accurately assessing them as a call to action. So you'd think that after learning the power of the pivot back in 2006 and continuously adapting over the years, I naturally would have applied that lesson in 2021 when I decided to launch a new tea company, right?

Wrong. Again.

———

The idea to enter the tea industry started to form after a conversation with bestselling author, podcast host, and former monk Jay Shetty. In 2018, I was a guest on his podcast to talk about the launch of my first book, *The Execution Factor*. From the moment we started chatting, it was as if the universe had conspired to bring two seemingly opposite individuals together. There I was, a fast-talking California tech entrepreneur, face-to-face with a former monk who had spent time sitting quietly with his thoughts at an ashram in India. On paper, we were as different as Silicon Valley and the Himalayas. But there was an instant connection, and we were so engaged in our hour-long chat that we barely noticed the producer signaling to us to wrap up.

"Let's continue this conversation over lunch," I suggested. And so, with members of our team, we enjoyed one of those meals where time seemed to stand still. We shared stories, laughed out loud, and discussed our passions. I found myself increasingly curious as Jay described his approach to holistic well-being and mindful living. To quote the movie *Casablanca*, it was the start of a beautiful friendship.

Fast-forward two years to February 2020, the month before the world locked down due to the pandemic. We were having dinner at Craig's in West Hollywood, and I was telling Jay and his wife, Radhi, about my new venture, 100.co, a technology company that uses cutting-edge artificial intelligence to create consumer products. As I explained how AI could be used to identify market gaps and consumer trends, Jay's face lit up. It turned out he and Radhi had been talking about creating a physical product.

"What kind of product did you have in mind?" I asked.

Jay smiled. "Something that's authentic to us. Something born from an everyday ritual we do together. We're thinking . . . tea."

Tea? At first, I was a bit taken aback. It seemed so traditional and antiquated. But as Jay passionately explained the concept—tea as a moment of connection, tea that inspires serenity, tea with ingredients that infuse wellness, tea that he and Radhi already drink as part of their families' ritual—I felt my skepticism melt away.

Radhi explained what made their approach so unique. "When Jay gets sick or when he's tired from traveling, I make tea blends from scratch with special adaptogens for healing. He calls me his master potion maker!"

"Why should I be the only one who benefits?" Jay asked.

With that, Radhi began painting the vision, inviting us to imagine a tea brand that was changing health habits. "Imagine a tea for body *and* mind," she said. "Packed with adaptogens—ashwagandha, lion's mane, reishi mushrooms—that allow you to incorporate wellness into an everyday ritual."

I'd heard enough. I was hooked. "Sounds amazing. Let's put it to the test." This was a perfect opportunity to use 100.co's AI to validate if there was a market opportunity. Turns out that tea was a sleeping giant—an industry ripe for disruption, a "sleepy" category crying out for innovation. Jay and Radhi's ritual of infusing their ordinary teas with adaptogens and nootropics was revolutionary. Tea 2.0.

We had all the ingredients for success, literally and figuratively. I brought years of experience as a seasoned entrepreneur who had started and scaled global businesses. Jay and Radhi brought their massive, engaged audience—more than 50 million followers strong, cultivated through Jay's number one wellness podcast *On Purpose*. In addition, Radhi brought her expertise as a plant-based Ayurvedic chef. As a trio, we brought passion, vision, and purpose.

Cut to September 2021 when SAMA Tea was launched with the brand tagline "This Moment Is Yours"—a message inspired by Jay and Radhi's cherished memories of sharing tea with their families and one another. A deliberate emphasis on how drinking tea can bring people together and create community.

We hired an all-star team with deep experience in bringing new brands to market, and everyone told me there was a trusted industry playbook to follow. All beverage companies had relied on the same go-to-market strategy, they said. As a novice, I followed the lead of the seasoned experts.

After months of countless formula iterations and tasting sessions, we created six unique flavors infused with adaptogens. It wasn't just a product; it was a piece of Jay and Radhi's British-Indian heritage, and they had poured their love of tea into every cup. The playbook we followed continued to govern everything, from product to strategy to marketing to media to product launch . . . and the launch was spectacular.

The press glowed with praise, each article more complimentary than the last. Customer reviews read like love letters to SAMA. And then came the triumphant moment that still gives me goose bumps—watching Jay appear on *The Ellen DeGeneres Show*. There he was, sitting next to Ellen as she held up a box of our tea, with an eight-foot photo of the product in the background. It was surreal, like watching a dream come to life. We couldn't have bought that level of advertising if we had tried. No wonder my cell phone blew up with congratulatory messages. My first experience of the tea industry couldn't have gone any better. I felt unstoppable. Everything seemed so perfectly aligned.

I didn't realize it at the time, but I was falling into the oldest trap in business: thinking I had it all figured out, based on the playbook for success. I can still hear the industry veterans now. "The playbook is already written. Just follow it."

That's exactly what I did. I stuck to the plan like it was carved in stone.

Big mistake.

––––––––––

As the months went by, reality started to sink in—people weren't drinking hot tea as quickly as we had hoped. Repeat orders were slow, we missed our revenue targets, and the money we were making wasn't sufficient to cover operational costs. Our vision for growth was at a crossroads. We hadn't quite stalled, but we were losing momentum. We had to reevaluate our plan.

We delved into researching high-growth categories and uncovered some valuable insight—ready-to-drink *functional* beverages were taking the market by storm—kombucha, probiotic drinks, and collagen-infused waters. Consumers couldn't drink enough! Ingredients like adaptogens and nootropics were used to boost mood, manage stress, and improve overall well-being, and the data projected that this corner of the market would skyrocket from $128 billion in 2021 to $200 billion by 2026.

We saw a golden opportunity: to expand into cold, adaptogenic, sparkling ready-to-drink tea—packaged in an aluminum can. This additional product line would help scale revenue growth. This wasn't reinvention; it was the pivot our product needed.

We dove into our product-expansion plans, crafted new formulas, and meticulously perfected the packaging for the cans. After dozens of formula iterations, we moved into production. But then we started hearing whispers about supply chain disruptions in a Covid world, and those whispers soon escalated into screaming news headlines: "COVID BREAKS SUPPLY CHAINS" and "GLOBAL SUPPLY CHAIN CRISIS."

Aluminum can prices didn't just rise, they exploded, rocketing by a staggering 67% practically overnight. Covid dramatically altered the entire landscape. Our ambitious plans for ready-to-drink tea in a can came to a sudden halt as a result of the high costs.

We felt blindsided.

For a few days, we toyed with the idea of using glass bottles, but they would prove too heavy (and, therefore, costly) to ship. The consensus was that we stick to the plan and ride out the storm. But this storm was simply too powerful to ride out. The market uncertainty froze all investor funding, leaving us unable to raise money. Cash was running low, yet we stubbornly clung to our original plan—a plan that relied on market conditions that no longer existed.

I knew if we didn't take action soon, we would run out of cash. I met with Jay and Radhi, delivering the news that felt like the worst-case scenario had become reality: "We need to scale back and go back to the drawing board."

My heart sank. We were right back where we started, just the three of us.

Given the dwindling cash, the only CEO the company could afford was . . . me. Mainly because my salary was $0. It wasn't the career move I'd envisioned, but I took on the challenge, motivated by a determination to launch our tea product, and, at some level, wanting to prove that business basics are consistent, regardless of industry. And the first thing I did? I threw that playbook out the window! I needed to trust my gut more and ditch the "this is how things are done" philosophy. We needed to be scrappy, creative, and resourceful.

The second thing I did was leverage my network to secure a strategic investor who would add an injection of cash to provide the runway we needed to bring our new ready-to-drink, canned tea to market.

We found an investor who shared our passion for tea, which is crucial in the early stages of a startup. Every investor needs to believe in the mission as deeply as you do.

The third action I took was to increase our prices. While I couldn't change the higher cost of aluminum, I *could* change our product pricing to cover those costs as well as the ingredients. We knew we needed to find a customer who was willing to pay a premium for a high-quality, organic product.

We set our sights on Erewhon, the upscale, health-focused, organic-only Los Angeles–based supermarket. Its shoppers don't just buy products—they're invested in the lifestyle that comes with them. Similarly, our tea offered more than just a beverage; it was a gateway to enhancing overall wellness. But when I bounced the Erewhon idea off a few people, I heard pretty much the same response: "There's no way you'll get in there . . . It's not going to happen . . . You can't get in there with no other retail presence."

There will always be people telling you why something can't be done, but their experience isn't your experience. Do what you need to do: knock on doors, make the calls, get creative, and be persistent. For me, responding to other people's doubts is all about mindset. You can focus on all the reasons something won't work, but that only creates self-imposed barriers and leads to inaction. As I always ask myself, "What's the worst that can happen?" and the answer in this case was that someone could say "no."

After getting nowhere in asking my network if anyone had a contact at Erewhon, I decided to pivot my approach by being a little more creative. Ask anyone who knows me; I'm relentless in pursuing all options. I won't take "no" for an answer until all paths, avenues, alleys, and dead ends have been exhausted.

I delivered a bright-blue Igloo cooler, filled with a six-pack of ready-to-drink SAMA, a sales sheet, and a handwritten note, to Erewhon's headquarters. It was a long shot but it couldn't hurt. And when I didn't hear anything for weeks, I assumed it hadn't worked.

Then, one day out of the blue, our new investor called with big news—she had landed a meeting with a top executive at Erewhon! Even better, this executive had seen the cooler, tried our tea, and loved it. Within weeks, Erewhon placed an order for our tea to be stocked in all 10 stores across Los Angeles, just in time for summer! We had secured a spot on the most coveted shelves in the grocery world, and we were ecstatic—it was the breakthrough we needed.

Everything was finally falling into place. I remember sitting at my desk, looking at the colorful, beautifully designed cans of SAMA lined up in front of me, wanting to pinch myself.

Then, just eight days before production was set to start, my phone rang—it was our company attorney. "Kim, we've received a cease-and-desist order from a company claiming they own the brand name," he said. "They're demanding that we stop using the name SAMA."

"How did this happen? How did we miss this?" I asked, struggling to stay composed as I spoke to my lawyer. By this point in my entrepreneurial journey, I was proud of my ability to roll with the punches, but this setback floored me. I had assumed the lawyers had carried out a thorough trademark search; they claimed they had, but someone clearly missed it.

I sat at my desk, looking at those same cans adorned with a name we now couldn't use. We couldn't pass up this opportunity to be in Erewhon and we were set to launch in two weeks. There was only one option—we had to pivot. New name it was.

Trademarking an original name can be challenging at the best of times, but the odds of securing a new name two weeks before a supermarket launch felt insurmountable, and we hadn't told Erewhon about this snag yet. Jay, Radhi, and I scribbled down ideas—we needed something fresh, exciting, and aligned with our brand personality. On top of that, because we didn't have time to overhaul the can design, we were limited to four letters. We sifted through thousands of names, and each one we liked was already taken.

With a week to go, we stumbled across "JOYO"—a name owned by a closed yogurt company that was happy to sell us the rights. We had secured a name that captured a positive, *joyo*us vibe and was 100% on brand.

All I had to do now was break the news to Erewhon. I was acutely aware that an eleventh-hour name change could expose our vulnerabilities as a startup, but luckily, they were incredibly understanding and showed genuine empathy for the late curveball we'd been thrown. Such rock-solid support was a powerful reminder of the importance of building strong partnerships in business.

With our new name JOYO approved and Erewhon fully aboard, we needed a way to introduce our brand to customers. So we decided to hit the road . . . literally. We got a branded JOYO truck to drive the streets of Los Angeles—a rolling billboard, a mobile tasting station, and a conversation starter all in one.

The JOYO roadshow traveled around the city, from Venice Beach to Santa Monica, from Beverly Hills to Calabasas. We gave out

T-shirts, the media covered every pit stop, and Jay and Radhi hosted a launch event at their home.

The brand awareness paid off. And Target placed a huge order to put JOYO in 1,400 of its stores *nationwide*. One of the biggest department stores in the United States wanted our sparkling tea on its shelves. After a series of setbacks, it finally felt like we were breaking through to the other side.

Then, I got a call from my lawyer—again.

"Kim, I'm afraid we've got another cease-and-desist letter. We can't use JOYO."

My phone almost dropped out of my hand. This must be a joke, right?

Wrong.

This time, a billion-dollar food company claimed that the name and colors were *too similar* to one of their tea products. While we disagreed, we didn't have the cash to fight against a well-known, deep-pocketed corporation; there was no way we would win.

I took a walk outside, overwhelmed with disbelief, wondering how on earth this kept happening. I was disheartened and, honestly, felt a bit defeated. Not great for an eternal optimist.

I called Jay and Radhi, telling them what had happened.

"Kim," said Jay, his voice calm and assured. "I know this is another setback, but we just need to change our name again, and I know it's worth it."

He launched into a passionate reminder of the vision we had started with—and how far we had come. And he was right, every obstacle and pivot had made our product and brand better.

Radhi chimed in. "We started this company to bring healthy choices to everyone. We can still do this."

That call was reinspiring and reenergizing and, as I hung up, I laughed to myself, fully understanding why Jay is one of the most booked inspirational speakers in the world. It also demonstrated the power of the pivot. Keep changing. Keep switching it up. Stay on your toes. Be nimble.

In business, there will always be problems. It doesn't matter what field you're in. The questions then become "Do you like the problem you're solving?" and "Do you like the people you're problem-solving with?" If the answer to either of those questions is "no," then it's going to be a long road. For me, the answers were "yes" and "YES!" I was intrigued by the beverage industry, and I loved working with Jay and Radhi.

So, once again, we pivoted—in search of a new name. Take three.

We used the reset as an opportunity to elevate the product. The more taste tests we conducted, the more consumers told us they wanted less sugar and lower calories. That's when we decided to reformulate to remove the fruit juice so that each can contained zero sugar and only five calories—another demonstration of a pivot making the product better.

To find the most meaningful name, Jay bounced around some more ideas and reflected on the "why" behind the product: the moments shared with his family making and enjoying the ritual. That's when he had his lightbulb moment: "JUNI."

"It's an acronym for Just You 'n' I!" he said.

We loved the new name. The focus groups loved it. And the customers clearly loved it, too, because when the revamped product returned to the shelves of Erewhon, our sales doubled. I remember standing in an Erewhon aisle, watching a shopper reach for a can, completely unaware of our chaotic journey that had led to that moment. She read the label and dropped it into her cart like it was the easiest decision in the world. The ultimate payoff for all our pivots. From that day, we never looked back. We started in 10 stores with JUNI, and we have since scaled to more than 3,000 stores across the United States!

Our willingness to pivot—to adapt, to evolve, to learn—didn't enable success. It *was* our success. The changes we made transformed JUNI from a struggling startup to a thriving beverage brand. Who knows, maybe we'll need to pivot again further down the line. Staying open to that possibility, rather than rigidly holding on to original plans, is a healthy approach in business. So my advice to you is to pivot and pivot again. Trust me, it will pay off.

The Five Pivots Every Leader Faces

Whether you're running a small startup, managing a large corporation, or overseeing a creative project, there will inevitably be times when you need to adjust your approach. Through numerous pivots in my career—particularly in the creation of JUNI—I've identified five key pivots most leaders face.

1. *The Product Pivot:* Switching from hot tea to cold tea in a can was a product pivot. This type of pivot requires a shift in your product offering in response to declining sales/revenue, consumer feedback, or an obstacle that prevents entry into the market. A classic example of a product pivot is Slack, the communication tool. It began in 2009 as an internal communication tool for a gaming startup: Tiny Speck. When its first game, *Glitch,* failed to attract enough players to make the business viable, they changed their offering entirely and instead focused on expanding into a corporate communication

tool. Five years later, Slack went public and is still one of the most popular tools for teams globally.

2. *The Market Pivot:* A market pivot is triggered by the economic climate, consumer trends, public health emergencies, or advances in technology. These days, I keep a close eye on any new technology, regarding it as my friend rather than my enemy. A great example today is AI and ChatGPT. Are you putting your head in the sand, hoping it's just a fad? Or are you embracing it as a tool for improving productivity? In a constantly changing environment, you have a decision to make: Stay stagnant or adapt.

3. *The People Pivot:* The people pivot can be the most emotionally difficult pivot to make. As companies grow, or scale back, they require different people with different skill sets. Having the courage to make tough decisions is crucial for success, and new leadership can lead to new growth strategies. A great example of a people pivot is Tesla. Elon Musk replaced the original founders and took over as CEO in 2008. Under his new leadership, Tesla pivoted from niche electric roadsters to mass-market electric vehicles, transforming the company into the global leader in EV technology.

4. *The Pricing Pivot:* When we switched to ready-to-drink tea and needed to cover higher aluminum costs, we raised our prices. We knew our target customer would pay a premium for an organic drink packed with adaptogens. You can also adjust the pricing to appeal to a wider audience. That's what Uber did. It initially began with premium pricing for a black car but later pivoted its price to a lower-cost option, UberX, to appeal to a broader market and therefore bring in more business.

5. *The Customer Pivot:* We first focused on hot tea enthusiasts but made a strategic customer pivot to target cold tea consumers.

While it may seem like the same market, the customer base is entirely different. By shifting our focus, we aligned our product with a more receptive market, driving growth and long-term success. Look at Shopify. It started as a platform selling snowboarding equipment before recognizing that other businesses needed e-commerce tools, so it pivoted to providing an e-commerce platform for small and medium-size businesses, and it became a global leader in online retail solutions.

Every pivot we made at JUNI was a step forward. Yet throughout all the changes, we held on to the mission that powered the brand. The name may have been different, but our vision and values remained the same. We stayed true to who we are while recognizing that we had to adopt a different strategy.

In a world where technology is always evolving, it's more important than ever that leaders pivot to ensure their success. It might mean making small changes. It might mean 180-degree switches. But when those times come, embrace the pivot. Let it be your superpower. Because what might feel like a crushing blow in the moment can actually be an opportunity in disguise, leading to fresh possibilities that help you to achieve long-term growth.

What Stops People from Pivoting?

Based on countless conversations I've had with leaders, executives, and investors over the years, there are two common factors that create resistance to change.

One is fear. Fear of making a wrong turn. Fear of going against the original plan. The other is ego. Being too proud to admit when something isn't working. Being too concerned that taking a new direction will lead others to question your capabilities.

There is often a mistaken belief that adopting a new plan is an admission of being "wrong," and people don't like being wrong. Personally, I'd rather be "wrong" and win than be "right" and lose. If you don't pivot when a change is needed, you'll be in danger of becoming the next Blockbuster video—failing to adapt and getting left behind.

Blockbuster was once the largest video rental company in the world, but it refused to pivot its business model. Instead of evolving, Blockbuster clung to its physical store model, where customers had to visit in person to rent movies. In sharp contrast, Netflix saw the future and responded proactively, pivoting from its mail-order business to a streaming model that revolutionized how we consume content today. Blockbuster's failure to pivot proved fatal, forcing them to file for bankruptcy in 2010 with a reported $1 billion debt.

The Blockbuster tale serves as a warning about the risks of being too rigid. Rapid changes in market trends can affect any industry, so even if your planning has been flawless and your customer base is strong, you should always monitor the pulse of new market trends. I dismissed the rise of social media in 2006 and had to scramble to catch up. So stay up to speed with all the latest market research and test your product with consumers as much as you can. As soon as you detect the landscape shifting, incorporate "the three R's" framework—rethink, reorganize, react.

Assess where you are and start working out how to pivot to meet the moment.

Remember, there is no shame in acknowledging you need to change. I work with many entrepreneurs who feel they can't deviate from the original plan given to investors. But investors like me understand that plans change—what matters is your ability as a leader to adapt and ensure that the business stays viable.

If I've learned anything, it's that nothing ever goes as planned. The key to survival and success is the ability to adapt and keep moving forward. We may resist pivoting due to fear, pride, a lack of the right people, or the absence of a new idea, but embracing change is what sets thriving businesses apart from those that fall behind.

Pivoting to Success

Knowing when and how to pivot greatly increases your odds of success. I've invested in more than 100 companies, and I'd say that 99 have pivoted at least once; many of them, multiple times.

Anyone can make a pivot. You don't need to be a CEO. Whenever you make a conscious decision to change course in life—to be more aligned with your values, your goals, or your soul's calling—you're embracing the pivot. New life, new beginnings, new opportunities. For some people, it can be as dramatic as finding a new job, in a new city, with a new romantic partner. For others it can look more like adjusting marketing strategy or adopting a new technology. Regardless of how big or small the pivot is, making space for something new often results in positive outcomes.

So I challenge you to stop and ask yourself: "What's the best pivot I've made?"

It's an insightful exercise to chart the pivots that led to major shifts in your life.

Grab a pen and paper and write down all the times you consciously changed direction and then think about how those pivots played out.

What changed for the better?

What successes or achievements did they lead to?

What did they teach you, then or later?

Pivoting can be scary because it usually involves a leap into the unknown. But if a strategic shift is executed well, it can be one of the most exciting and rewarding ways to propel your business, or life, toward long-term success. And if a pivot doesn't work out and forces another pivot, embrace the journey and keep changing, just as we had to with JUNI. We navigated through one setback after another, and the power of the pivot allowed us to end up exactly where we were meant to be.

LESSON <small>IN THE</small> MISTAKE

The willingness to pivot isn't just a skill—it's a competitive edge. The real mistake isn't having to pivot; it's resisting the pivot until you have no other choice.

CHAPTER SUMMARY

Self-reflection: When faced with unexpected challenges, do you find your-self clinging to the original plan, or are you open to reassessing? Are there areas in your life today where you should consider pivoting?

Key Takeaways:

▶   **The Power of Adaptability:** Be prepared to admit when something isn't working. Being too attached to a plan can be to your detriment. The ability to change direction is crucial for survival and growth. Adapting to change rather than sticking rigidly to original plans helps overcome challenges and new opportunities.

▶   **The Three *R*'s Framework:** To help quickly assess next steps and what a potential pivot looks like, use the rethink, reorganize, and react framework. When you do, you'll make thoughtful decisions, take timely action, and avoid setbacks.

▶   **The Five Key Pivots to Recognize:** The willingness and ability to pivot can be your superpower, and every leader needs to know the five most common pivots—product, market, people, pricing, and customer. Each one requires a new strategy, whether it's adapting to new conditions, changing the target market, or restructuring the team. Identify the pivot your life and business need, then take action to make it happen.

▶   **Find Opportunities in Challenges:** Each pivot is an opportunity to reset. What may initially seem like a setback can become an opportunity for innovation. Being open to change allows you to turn obstacles into strategic advantages, leading to long-term growth.

▶   **Stay Informed to Stay Ahead:** Rigid thinking can prevent you from making necessary pivots. Stay informed. Keep an eye on market trends. Embrace a mindset of continuous learning that will enable you to adapt, thrive, and be agile. Recognize that the decision to pivot–and taking action on it–is a reflection of strength, not a sign of weakness.

Millionaire Mindset: I view the ability to pivot as a powerful mindset for growth. I trust in my ability to adapt and to make bold moves without letting fear or pride hold me back. I believe every pivot opens the door to new opportunities.

MISTAKE #7

Picking the Wrong People

*First impressions are like movie trailers—they showcase
the highlights but conceal the flaws. I learned this the hard
way when I hired someone who was perfect on paper
and full of charm. This mistake cost me millions.*

Have you ever met that "perfect person," the one you were convinced would be a complete game changer? Whether it's a significant other, a friend, a roommate, a business partner, or a new hire, there's no escaping the instant connection, the undeniable magnetism, and the effortless chemistry. You can't help but think, *Where has this person been all my life?*

It's happened to me a few times—when I met my husband, when I met my college best friend, and when I met a podcast host who became my business partner. I felt they were destined to be in my life. And there is power in that, but there's also danger.

The danger lurks when we confuse an authentic, deep connection with a connection that is superficial. The ability to distinguish between these two is an invaluable skill, though it can be difficult to master.

I know this all too well. I've hired the wrong employees, part-nered with the wrong individuals, and invested in the wrong found-ers. Why did I make these mistakes? Because I was so captivated by their "halo glow" that I missed the warning signs right in front of me.

Take the case of Mark.

My multimillion-dollar tech company was growing rapidly, and the pressure from the board to keep scaling revenue was intense. With an ambitious target set for the year, hitting those numbers would be impossible without a head of sales. I searched high and low for the perfect candidate, but a six-month search proved fruitless. Against that backdrop, on a cold, snowy day in December in New York, I met Mark for coffee at a cafe in Grand Central Station.

Right off the bat, I liked him. Immaculately dressed in crisp blue shirt, well-fitted jacket, and dark jeans, he conveyed an air of professionalism and approachability, topped off with charisma and confidence. Talking to him felt "familiar," like two old friends recon-necting after a long time apart. He said all the right things about building a team, his love of technology, and his passion for people. At the end of our two hours together, it felt like this was the person we had been waiting for.

Afterward, I met my husband for dinner. "So, what did you think of Mark? What's his story?" John asked.

I paused, realizing that I'd barely scratched the surface of his career history, despite our engrossing conversation. But, in my enthu-siasm, I neglected to dig deeper into his experience and the reasons behind his decision to leave his current job—misstep number one in a larger mistake.

"You know, I think he's exactly what we need," I said, finding reassurance in the facts from his resume. He'd led high-performing teams, worked with some of the top brands in the space, and con-sistently exceeded sales targets. "It's serendipitous. He's perfect." I ordered a celebratory glass of champagne and breathed a sigh of relief. Finally, I had found my head of sales.

A few weeks later, after a second interview, I hired Mark. On his first day, he stepped into the conference room to meet a sales team eager for a leader. He listened intently and painted a vision that had everyone fully engaged. I walked away confident, trusting that the team was in safe hands.

In the first month of Mark's tenure, he hit the ground running, conducting in-depth, one-on-one meetings with each team member, identifying opportunities ripe for early wins, and implementing a new customer outreach process that strengthened existing relationships. Revenues increased across several accounts in his first 30 days.

And then everything started to unravel. One of our sales reps expressed concern that while Mark made bold statements about his vision, he always sidestepped questions when asked about the finer details, such as deliverables, benchmarks, and tactics. *Well, not everyone can have all the answers while still getting up to speed*, I rationalized.

But within the next two weeks, he missed a crucial sales call, canceled two of our one-on-one meetings, and was late in sharing his sales projections. There was no disregarding the red flags.

When I asked him directly, he apologized and said his son was sick; he promised he would stay on top of the priorities moving forward. I expressed genuine sympathy but made clear that I'd be holding him accountable; too much was at stake. As he left my office, I felt uneasy. My intuition was trying to speak to me, but I chose not to listen.

Sure enough, Mark was late to another one-on-one with me the next week. When he finally arrived at my office, he said the meeting had "fallen off his calendar." He looked like a shadow of the man I hired. Exhausted. Zero confidence. And coming across a little scattered, as if his mind were elsewhere. When I probed a little deeper to see what was really going on and if there was anything I could do to help, he seemed almost defensive.

"You've been supportive, Kim," he said. "There are some hard things going on in my personal life that have been weighing on me . . . things I'm not ready to talk about."

The seriousness in his tone created a barrier all on its own; he wasn't going to let me in. *Was his son still sick? Was his marriage on the rocks? Was this a mental health issue?* I genuinely felt terrible for him, and I wanted to support him through this hard time.

People would later ask why I didn't cut my losses there and then. The answer is that it's hard for me to give up on people. Red flags might well be warning signs, but they can also be turned into teachable moments. Maybe someone needs more time. Maybe they require more resources or training. Maybe they will bounce back. When it came to Mark, my "maybes" worked overtime. That said, I was also running the company and overseeing a complex acquisition. I didn't have the time to micromanage everything.

There was no escaping the fact that I made excuses for Mark, hoping he would turn things around. That mistake didn't just affect me—it impacted my entire team.

Looking back, I realize that I didn't fully grasp my own issues— choosing the path of least resistance and avoiding confrontation. Maybe I wasn't ready to admit that I had made a bad hire. But the truth about avoidance is that you're just sweeping something under the rug until it becomes a giant lump that can't be covered up any longer. Avoidance only delays the inevitable . . . and the inevitable eventually happened with Mark.

As well as continuing to miss critical meetings and pitches, I later found out he seldom answered emails. The final straw was when I learned he had skipped three meetings with a direct report who was waiting on him to approve three client proposals. My team was constantly disappointed, deadlines were missed, launches were delayed, and my empathy quickly turned to frustration. I'd had enough.

Mark's issues had started as small, barely noticeable cracks. But as the pressure for revenue growth intensified, those cracks became gaping sinkholes that impacted everyone. As much empathy as I felt, it was clear he had deeper problems beyond my ability to help. I finally made the decision to let him go.

By going through that experience and taking full ownership of my role in it, I gained invaluable lessons. Now, with the goal of steering you away from the same minefield, let's break down the pitfalls of picking the wrong people I fell into.

The Cost of Picking the Wrong People

Choosing the wrong person for a role is like building a house on a shaky foundation—the exterior might look impressive and sturdy, but, as time goes on, cracks start to form and the whole structure starts to wobble. The bigger the role, the bigger the impact. Unfortunately, this scenario is all too common in business. Nearly half of all new hires fail within the first 18 months.[25]

The resulting cost can be extensive in terms of time, productivity, team morale, and, of course, money. I made excuses and shied away from conflict because I didn't want to face the cost of my own mistake.

With Mark gone, the consequence of my mistake wasn't just visible—it was unavoidable. There was a massive leadership gap, and it had my name on it. I had no choice but to step in. That meant running the company and taking over as head of sales. Did I have time for this? Absolutely not. But part of owning a mistake is making time for the mess it created.

And the mess was staggering. We were millions away from hitting our quarterly budget. Mark had not only failed to drive sales, he had actively damaged client relationships by not responding to their calls. I flew across the country to meet with multiple clients, trying to salvage them. Some relationships were beyond repair. Others were willing to give us another shot but only under one condition: that we deliver results, and that it would never happen again.

Meanwhile, I had an exhausted, demoralized team who had spent months picking up the slack. They were tired. They were disenchanted. And before I asked them to lean in harder than ever, I owed them something first—an apology. I gathered the team and admitted what they already knew: I had picked the wrong person. I hadn't stepped in soon enough when they had told me how bad things were. I told them I saw how much weight they had been carrying and that I was taking full responsibility. This wasn't on them. It was on me.

And then, I asked them for one more push.

They clocked 12-hour days as pizza boxes piled up in the conference room. I rolled up my sleeves and got in the trenches with them—joining late-night strategy sessions, jumping on client calls, and making sure they knew they weren't alone in the fight.

We gave it 110%, but we *still* missed our numbers.

That was the real consequence. No amount of hard work could undo the damage done. We had lost momentum, revenue, and, most importantly, trust. I try not to dwell on past mistakes, but this one? It cost us millions. And not just in lost revenue. The average cost of replacing a C-level executive is twice their salary. Add in lost time, reduced team productivity, and emotional exhaustion, and the impact becomes even more significant.

Get it wrong with startups, and the consequences can be felt even more deeply. According to *Harvard Business Review*, poor hiring is linked to 60% of startup failures.[26] The cost of picking the wrong person isn't just financial. It's cultural. It's emotional. It's the difference between a company that thrives and one that barely survives.

The Four Pitfalls When Picking People

My failure in hiring Mark was undeniable, and I had to act fast to find a replacement. We needed leadership and didn't have time to spare. But I wasn't going to allow myself to make the same mistake again. I learned a critical lesson—taking the time to thoroughly evaluate a candidate (or partner) is essential, not just for their experience but also for their character.

In an interview, people will always showcase why they are the ideal fit; they may well oversell themselves. It's on the interviewer to do their due diligence, dig deeper, and uncover any potential red flags or concerns.

I had been persuaded by the combination of subtle swagger and charm that made Mark appear confident, competent, and likable—important qualities for a sales leadership role. He did a great job of selling himself; he was a salesperson after all!

On my part, I didn't do a great job of having a substantive conversation about Mark's history and missed red flags at the second interview. He spoke about his sales successes but couldn't give specific examples because of the nature of "the confidential projects." He also said that the top clients he had previously worked with were no longer in that role, which made it impossible for me to verify his references. I believed the polished resume and the person in front of me were telling the truth, and I paid the price for that naivete.

For all future hires—and I've kept to this ever since—I would rely on a gentle interrogation about their experience, values, skills, and character. If there were an iota of doubt, any missing information, or any holes in their story, I would not move forward. I also developed a hiring framework so I could remind myself of all the nonnegotiables. I called it "the four pitfalls when picking the right people." Now, when I'm choosing new people in any aspect of my life, I keep these pitfalls front of mind.

1. POP–Perfect on Paper

The perfect-on-paper types represent one of the most significant pitfalls I've encountered. Anyone who's familiar with the dating scene might recognize this pitfall, too. Everything about them seems perfect—the bio on the dating app, the messages they send, even the rave review of a friend setting you up. It's easy to be swayed by the perception of perfection. Then the whole fantasy comes crashing down when you meet in person—or a few weeks down the line when the first impressions mask starts to slip. The illusions play out the same way in business, too.

I've seen a few dazzling resumes in my time from candidates who worked at top companies in their field, notched up notable accomplishments, and had lists of impressive degrees. And then the interview itself didn't match the hype.

In business or life, we can all relate to falling for the POPs—Perfect on Paper. Many of us have learned that if someone seems too good to be true, they often are! The more perfect they appear, the more important it is to dig deeper.

My recommendation for avoiding this pitfall is to view the process as an archaeological dig. The details on the resume provide only the most superficial layer. You need to excavate another three or four layers to unearth the real person concealed behind the interview persona.

The key to this excavation is to have a robust screening process, and that includes asking interview questions that can't be easily glossed over or danced around. Rely on classic, open-ended questions to extract more expansive answers. Once I've warmed up the interviewee, here are the questions I often ask:

1. *Who was your most difficult boss? Why?*
2. *Tell me about a time you failed and what that felt like.*

3. *What talent, skill, or attribute do you think sets you apart? What trait do you have that others do not always recognize?*

4. *What would I learn about you three months from now that I couldn't learn in an interview?*

5. *If we were in a room full of your ex-colleagues, and we asked them the one thing they would want to change about you, what would they say?* Then ask, *Have you done anything to change that?*

6. [Save this as your last question.] *Who do you most admire and respect, living or dead? Why?* [Really listen to the "why." The answer often reveals the traits and core values they either possess or aspire to develop.]

These are not general questions that allow a candidate to provide an overview or philosophize; these questions are designed to extract personal insight that will speak to their attitude, values, emotional maturity, and perspective on life. In turn, their telling answers should raise more questions that allow the conversation to keep moving naturally. Should you be faced with any defensiveness or lack of transparency (as I faced with Mark), that in itself is important information.

Remember to go beyond accomplishments and accolades. Pose hypothetical situations that the candidate might encounter on the job. Don't simply ask about their actions; ask what motivated their actions. Don't ask what their solution to a problem would be; ask about the thought process behind it. Having a tool kit of thought-provoking questions can be illuminating, revealing attributes and qualities that may otherwise have been concealed. Most importantly, you will see the candidate with more clarity, allowing you to reach a more informed decision.

2. Picking Under Pressure

Hiring under pressure is like grocery shopping when hungry. You head to the store to grab some salmon and greens but end up impulse buying a bag of chips and a pint of that Italian gelato you can't resist.

Many times in business, you'll be shopping for the right hire at a time when you are drowning in work, or have limited bandwidth, or when circumstances are applying a sense of urgency. Keeping a calm head and stepping away from all the emotion and stress is imperative. Otherwise, you risk hurrying a decision, making a hasty hire, and picking a "pretty good" candidate just to take the load off, instead of waiting to find a better one. I was guilty of that with Mark, feeling not only the pressure from the board but my own self-imposed pressure after spending time interviewing other candidates and getting nowhere.

More than half of C-suite executives say that hiring in a hurry leads to a bad hire.[27] And after sharing my disastrous head-of-sales story with several peers, I heard some crazy stories of hiring hell that reassured me I wasn't alone.

No matter how much pressure you feel, it's important to take a breath, zoom out, and step away from all the swirling emotions that stress can bring. If you pay close attention to what you are feeling and thinking, you'll know whether the pressure is getting to you or not. And if it is, that's okay. Simply being aware of that fact can be enough, because you know not to make a decision from such a reactive place. It's okay to feel pressure as long as you're not making a rash decision simply to alleviate it. If you feel stressed about making a hire, imagine the stress that comes with the fallout of making a wrong hire. Don't react to what's going on around you. Respond to the highest standards the job demands. Trust me—you can't afford for a mis-hire to turn into a bigger misfire.

3. The Bias Blind Spot

I know of a once-vibrant tech company in San Francisco that was growing fast. In the space of three years, it had tripled its revenue, attracted millions of dollars from investors, and couldn't hire engineers and product managers fast enough. One role it needed to fill was head of product, and a standout candidate ticked a lot of boxes.

He had previously worked at the same company as one of the other execs, he supported the same football team as one of the co-founders, and he had mutual friends with at least two existing employees (and came highly recommended). Those factors played a part in him ultimately landing the job, and it's a classic example of the bias blind spot pitfall. It's when we don't bring true scrutiny to the table because all we can see is the common ground, the shared passions, and the similar background.

Within six months, the mis-hire misfired when six female colleagues made complaints about his flirtatious behavior. A tightly knit team at a thriving startup now had to deal with a wrench in the works that was undermining morale and affecting a prized work culture. The new head of product lasted less than a year, and that example goes to show how we need to toss out any bias, adopt impartiality, and bring rigor to the interview process, without fear or favor.

I confess that I've fallen into this pitfall. I've often found myself impressed by candidates who attended my same university, grew up in my hometown, had similar hobbies, or followed a similar career path. Subconsciously, I perceived these similarities as indicators of a "good fit," even if the individual didn't have the strongest qualifications among applicants. To become more objective and to refine my hiring process, I ushered in a more structured approach, based on four criteria to ensure that my decisions were focused on the essential qualities required for the role:

- A proven track record of productivity/efficiency in chosen field
- Adaptability as a problem-solver who finds creative solutions
- Strong alignment with the company's core values and culture
- Proven capability of operating at a high leadership level

This approach has helped me stay true to the needs of the position. If someone didn't meet the core requirements, I wouldn't consider them. What's more, to reinforce this discipline, I shared my nonnegotiable list with a trusted colleague who would conduct their own interviews, making sure I stayed accountable to the criteria. This second opinion was invaluable because on more than one occasion, it caught potential areas of concern that I missed. Not only has this method improved the quality of my hires, but it has also underscored the importance of maintaining high standards, even when faced with charismatic candidates and common ground.

4. Listen to Your Gut

As mentioned earlier, our gut instinct is one of the most underrated, underused skills we all have. It's the most reliable inner guidance system at our disposal. I listen to my gut all the time—so much so that I consider it one of my most trusted advisers. Let me explain why.

I was about to make a significant acquisition of a technology company. On paper, the deal seemed perfect. Numerous meetings were lined up with the CEO and the team. Every question I had was answered, every detail provided. But something in my gut told me to wait and reconsider. There was no rational explanation for my hesitation, but I felt a persistent, uneasy feeling . . . and I heeded that internal flare. I paused the acquisition. A short while later, it transpired that the company had lost a huge client, which dramatically affected its financial position. My inexplicable gut feeling had saved me from making a potentially costly mistake.

On the flip side, there was a pending deal where everything seemed uncertain, and my logical thinking told me to play it safe, but my intuition signaled otherwise. Something urged me to take a bold leap and partner with an up-and-coming company. It turned out to be one of my smarter calls. With our synergies, combined forces, and shared talent, our revenue exponentially increased.

Learning to listen to your gut isn't always easy, but, with practice, you can start to tune in to your body and how your intuition makes itself known. If you can hone and harness only one superpower, make it your intuition. And remember to listen when you're hiring someone who looks good on paper but your gut feels uneasy! It's a signal that on some level, there's an issue that requires closer attention.

The Right People Power Success

Picking the right people fuels your success. It's why finding the right fit is essential, not only for revenue and productivity but also for a thriving work culture.

In the aftermath of Mark's departure, I spent three months interviewing dozens of people, taking my time and adopting my new framework, digging into each candidate's capabilities and strengths. Ultimately, I hired Stacy, who came highly recommended by a trusted business partner, and it didn't take long to see why. Her strategic thinking and positive energy were matched by an ability to connect with people on a personal level; it was impressive to see how quickly she fostered a collaborative environment that inspired everyone. Unlike Mark, Stacy was someone whose first impressions were supported by the effective actions she took; she was a confident leader who brought out the best in people.

She didn't come in and make changes for the sake of change—she listened, observed, and implemented thoughtful, effective strategies. She not only met my expectations but exceeded them. Good on paper. Even better in reality.

I remember the day she walked into my office with a big smile on her face, not saying anything, even as she placed a sheet of paper on the desk in front of me.

"What's this?" I said.

She still said nothing as I unfolded the paper.

It was a purchase order, confirming that we had landed a new contract worth seven figures! We were going to hit our numbers and then some. The scream of joy that came out of my mouth that day echoed throughout the whole office. To celebrate, Stacy organized our first team happy hour in months, and the room buzzed with renewed excitement.

Stacy proved to be the missing link our team had needed all along. Our team meetings became more energized, employees were noticeably more motivated, and every action aligned with a clear vision backed by a solid strategy. She elevated our entire organization, which is what the best hires do. They don't just meet expectations, they redefine what is possible.

Picking the Right People Is a Success Multiplier

When you pick the right people, the resulting formula looks more like $1 + 1 = 3$ than $1 + 1 = 2$. What they bring to the team isn't just additive; it's a success multiplier. Choosing the right person in Stacy didn't just make my company millions—it brought a level of confidence and peace of mind that was invaluable.

In both business and life, the cost of picking the wrong people can be catastrophic, both financially and emotionally. As I learned from my experience with Mark, the ripple effects can disrupt your team, crush morale, and drain resources. But the deeper lesson is that we must recognize the pitfalls that lead to these missteps. Whether it's being swayed by someone who's perfect on paper, or making rushed decisions under pressure, overlooking bias, or ignoring a gut feeling, the consequences of these mistakes are significant.

The ability to evaluate people thoughtfully and objectively is crucial for success. As author Jim Collins says in his book *Good to Great*, "People are not your most important asset. The *right* people are."

LESSON IN THE MISTAKE

People who overpromise
rarely overdeliver. Red
flags don't fix themselves.
The sooner you address the
warning signs, the sooner
you prevent a mistake from
turning into a crisis.

CHAPTER SUMMARY

Self-reflection: When in your life have you fallen into the pitfall of picking the wrong person? What were the warning signs you missed? What lessons can you apply to future relationships?

Key Takeaways:

▶ **Beware of "Perfect on Paper":** First impressions can be misleading, especially if someone seems "perfect" at a glance. Look beyond the resume and dig deeper into personal values and real-life experiences.

▶ **Trust Your Gut Instinct:** Intuition is a powerful tool in decision-making, often revealing red flags that logical analysis alone may miss. Pay attention to gut feelings.

▶ **Check Your Bias Blind Spot:** Recognize the tendency to lean toward people who share common interests or backgrounds. Staying objective and obtaining second opinions can help prevent bias and ensure you're choosing the right person.

▶ **Do Your Due Diligence:** Poor hires account for 60% of startup failures. Don't make decisions under pressure. Zoom out. Be patient. Take the time to thoroughly assess a candidate.

▶ **The Right People Multiply Success:** Choosing the right people doesn't just add value; it multiplies it. The best people inspire, energize, and enhance overall performance, leading to greater productivity and profit.

Millionaire Mindset: I attract and choose the right people who align with my vision and align with my values. I am committed to finding individuals who are inspiring, energizing, and support my success.

MISTAKE #8

Believing You're Underqualified

My biggest regrets aren't from my mistakes but from the opportunities I let slip away due to self-doubt. I trusted my insecurities more than my potential.

When I was a senior in college, I landed a job at a small Beverly Hills marketing agency. It wasn't part of some master career plan—I simply needed money to pay for my meals and car payments. Six months into the role, I surprised everyone, including myself, by being asked to manage some of our biggest clients, which meant crafting compelling pitches and preparing detailed reports. Not bad for a 21-year-old who was simultaneously cramming for finals and pulling all-nighters to finish group projects.

Then came a conversation that would reframe how I saw my self-worth for the next decade.

My boss asked for a quiet word in his office. "Do me a favor," he said. "Don't tell anyone your age." I didn't know how to respond, and he must have read my confusion. "Look," he continued, "you're doing fantastic work. The clients love you, the numbers are great, and we'd like to promote you to lead our client services team, but"—he paused, choosing his words carefully—"it'll be easier if we tell the team you're twenty-eight and have more experience under your belt."

A 21-year-old man would never have been asked to do the same; he would have been celebrated as an up-and-coming talent. But as a woman, I was expected to lie about my age in order to make sure that the more senior people felt comfortable with me in a leadership role. The message was clear: My age and "lack of experience" were liabilities to be concealed, not achievements to be celebrated.

I agreed to pretend I was seven years older than I actually was and, looking back, that was a big mistake. I let the weight of my boss's seniority overshadow my instincts. I knew it was wrong but gave in when I should have stood my ground. I didn't fight for what was right. Worst of all, I didn't fight for myself. The thing about your early 20s is that you're still figuring yourself out, still learning to trust your gut. When an authority figure suggests you need to be something different in order to succeed, you tend to listen.

It seemed a small thing to me at the time, a little white lie about my age. But it reinforced a destructive mindset: that my actual experience, my real accomplishments, weren't enough. That my success needed a costume to be believable.

Fast-forward 10 years. I had sold my company, Frontline. I was running Adconion Direct and actively investing in LA startups. On paper, things looked great. I was scaling a global company and building a reputation as a prominent investor in the tech ecosystem. But that old voice of doubt had a way of showing up at the most inconvenient moments.

One of the companies I invested in had closed a massive funding round and offered me an opportunity to join the board of directors. Instead of seeing it as validation of my experience and worth, I only saw all the reasons why I was underqualified for such a position.

I pictured myself walking into that boardroom—the only woman, the *youngest* person at the table by decades, surrounded by gray-haired men with Ivy League MBAs and decades of superior experience. In my mind, I was that 21-year-old again, being told no one would take her seriously. I felt out of my depth and certain they'd quickly realize it.

So I turned down the offer.

A few years later, I happened to have dinner with one of the board members at a tech conference in Santa Monica, and, as we reminisced over old times, he asked why I'd declined the board seat years earlier. I told him the truth: I didn't believe I had enough experience as an investor and felt underqualified to be on the board.

He looked genuinely surprised. "Kim, we wanted you *precisely because* of your operating experience. We needed someone like you who had built and run a successful company in the digital advertising space. And we valued that you would bring a unique perspective to the table."

Now I was the one who was genuinely surprised. The irony hit me like a ton of bricks. The very things I thought made me underqualified were what made me a perfect fit for the role. I had completely misjudged the situation and, driven by an old echo from my agency days, I denied myself a seat on the board. I could have kicked myself. My mistake wasn't being young, female, or inexperienced—it was believing that those things somehow made me less qualified.

That night, I drove home from dinner past the same Beverly Hills streets where my office had been a decade earlier, as if I were traveling back in time. It was surreal to reflect on how far I had come. In that moment, I made myself a promise: I would never again let my insecurities lead me to self-reject. The next time an opportunity came—*especially* one that made me question if I was qualified enough—I would say "yes" and figure it out later.

Years later, another board opportunity for a fast-growing technology company came my way. This time, I didn't hesitate—I said "yes."

When I entered the boardroom for the first time, I wasn't just walking into a meeting—I was stepping into an entirely new world. I was surrounded by prominent venture capitalists and the most power-ful decision-makers in the industry.

And now, I had a seat at the table.

Every meeting was a master class in high-stakes decision-making. I wasn't just observing deals happen, I was participating inside the room where they were negotiated, structured, and implemented. It was nothing short of exhilarating. I learned about corporate risk, cor-porate governance, compensation committees, and how power moves are made at the highest levels.

It felt empowering to finally own my value. My years as an opera-tor gave me insights that other board members didn't have. They knew exits; I knew execution. They understood capital allocation, and I inti-mately understood the grind of building something from nothing. I saw myself the way they saw me—not as someone lucky to be there but as someone who belonged. My first board seat didn't just change my career, it changed my perspective on what I was capable of. Saying "yes" wasn't just about joining a board. It was about finally stepping into the room I should have been in all along.

The Invisible Chains of Self-Doubt

Can you think of a time you passed up an opportunity because you felt underqualified? Have you ever avoided speaking up in a meeting because you doubted yourself? Don't worry. You're not alone—I've read numerous articles that say 85% of people acknowledge that doubt has held them back from pursuing an opportunity at least once in their lives. If that statistic demonstrates anything, it's how so many of us battle the doubting mind.

Self-doubt fuels a sense of inadequacy, and it doesn't only affect people at the start of their career or when launching something new.

Countless talented people, even those at the top, struggle with self-doubt and wonder if they truly deserve their success. This is what self-sabotage does—it sows doubt even when you've achieved great things or acquired impressive accolades. It can make you feel as if you're undeserving, and that your limitations will soon be exposed and you'll be "found out."

Here's what you have to understand about self-doubt—it's just your ego talking. Whenever we decide to put our talent and abilities on the line, the ego fiercely defends our image of competence and capability. We might *want* to ask for a raise at work or apply for a new job, but we hesitate due to worries about being underqualified. That's because the ego's job is to safeguard our pride and self-esteem. It considers anything new or unfamiliar to be risky.

It's the same reason why people cling to the bar rather than take to the dance floor, why not all partygoers rush to the mic at karaoke, and why the prospect of public speaking can be terrifying to some. The ego tries to protect us from situations where we may look foolish or out of our depth.

No one explains it better than philosopher and author Rupert Spira: "Whenever we go beyond our limits, the ego experiences a little death because it is defined by its limits." But doubt only "exists on the surface of the mind," he says, so our task is to access our deeper truth and intuition. As he suggests: "Don't listen to the doubt. Listen to what your heart is telling you."

It's not uncommon for high achievers to feel unworthy of their accomplishments. Take former Facebook/Meta COO Sheryl Sandberg, one of the most influential figures in tech. A self-made billionaire, she began as a World Bank economist after earning her Harvard MBA, later leading online sales at Google before joining Facebook. In 2011, it all culminated in her being ranked fifth—ahead of First Lady

Michelle Obama—on the "World's 100 Most Powerful Women" list released annually by *Forbes*.

And yet behind that commanding exterior and laundry list of accolades, she struggled with believing she was a fraud. Sheryl was embarrassed about making the *Forbes* list. She felt "embarrassed and exposed," to the extent that when friends posted about it on their Facebook pages, she asked them to take it down, not feeling deserving of the honor. She thought all the fuss was "absurd" and "silly," she wrote in her book *Lean In*.

Doubt spares nobody. From CEOs to VPs, from first-time business owners to veteran entrepreneurs, from professional athletes to Oscar-winning actors. No matter how high you climb, self-doubt will climb alongside you. It affects people at every level. You might find yourself not speaking up in meetings, not sharing your ideas at brainstorming sessions, or not pushing for a deserved pay raise. You may have all the knowledge, but self-doubt will keep you silent and unseen.

It's perfectly natural to experience self-doubt, in the same way it's okay to experience fear. Where fear heightens your alertness to evaluate risk, doubt creates a pause to weigh your abilities and capabilities. If you're about to do a cliff dive into the ocean, for example, and all you've ever achieved is a belly flop from the 10-foot board at the local pool, self-doubt can serve as a wise reminder to maybe step back and reassess. But it becomes a problem when self-doubt is viewed as a true reflection of your ability.

You can't sit in self-doubt and make it your base camp; no one climbs mountains from that kind of start. Your base camp needs to be a solid structure built out of belief and sustained by confidence. Set up your base camp properly, and no amount of doubt will be able to stop you from reaching the summit.

The Three Faces of Doubt

Doubt isn't always a reflection of the truth. Picture yourself walking through a house of mirrors at a carnival. Each reflection shows a slightly different version of you—some stretch you to be taller than a tree, some squish you into a human bowling ball, most distort you to barely recognize yourself. Self-doubt works in the same way. It warps how we perceive ourselves. Instead of affirming the good things that are right in front of us, it leaves us questioning ourselves. I've encountered three different faces that doubt wears depending on the situation.

1. The Face of the Imposter

When we look in the mirror during moments of opportunity, the face that often stares back is that of an imposter.

After costing myself a seat on that corporate board, I never again talked myself out of an opportunity. But that didn't stop me from experiencing imposter syndrome—that limiting belief that makes us feel like other people will think we're a "fraud." I'm sure we can all relate to those times when we feel like an imposter in our own life, when we discount our intelligence, experience, or talents, and when we attribute our success to timing or luck.

Women grapple with this tendency the most. I see it in those I mentor and advise. They are more reluctant to apply for leadership positions, ask for raises, and pitch their business ideas. In 15 years as an angel investor, 90% of the pitch decks that I receive come from men. That's not because there aren't women creating incredible companies; it's because they hold back from reaching out.

When I ask the female founders why they didn't contact me sooner, the answer is usually tied to self-rejection. Countless times

I've heard "I didn't think you'd be interested because I don't have a lot of experience," or "I didn't think I was ready," or "I wanted to wait until I had more traction."

In fact, the term "imposter syndrome" was first coined in 1978 by two female psychologists whose work focused on high-achieving women.[28] But while women tend to feel it more acutely, some of the most outwardly confident men I know have confessed to me that they're constantly waiting for someone to tap them on the shoulder and say, "Sorry, there's been a terrible mistake." The truth is that most of us are pretty talented at keeping up appearances while privately feeling like a fraud.

Just ask Tom Hanks. Even though he's got shelves lined with Oscars, Golden Globes, and Emmys, he has struggled with imposter syndrome. "There comes a point where you think 'How did I get here? When are they going to discover that I am, in fact, a fraud and take everything away from me?'" he said in a radio interview with NPR.

When I look back at my career, I can chart the points on the map where doubt has been the loudest voice in my head, and it coincided with the precise points where I've grown the most. Whether launching my first company with zero experience, pitching to prominent investors, or venturing into an entirely new industry with JUNI, doubt made me question my capabilities. Why? Because I was stepping into new territory, venturing beyond anything my ego had ever experienced. In response, the ego tried to protect me by pulling me back. But these were the times when I needed to push through the doubt and grow.

Doubt will always seek to mislead you. If you've ever felt insecure about your education, doubt will tell you you're not smart enough. If you've questioned your abilities, doubt will mock your dream. If finances have ever been a struggle, doubt will say you don't deserve wealth. If you've worried about embarrassing yourself, doubt will say you're going to look foolish. If you've ever felt overlooked, doubt will insist you don't belong in the spotlight. And if you listen to those doubts, you're less likely to take risks, pursue a dream, ask for a promotion, negotiate a higher salary, or start something new.

2. The Face of Comparison

Growing up, I never felt like I was smart. I struggled in school and constantly compared myself with my twin sister. How could I not? Genetically we shared the same DNA. I spent my childhood wrestling with this feeling of comparison. I can remember one friend joking, "Guess you're not the smart one"—words that would haunt me. Decades later, as a parent of two sets of twins, I see that same dynamic play out daily. Watching them play and compete, I'm reminded of how natural and deeply ingrained comparison can be.

Comparison is something every person on Earth deals with, not just twins. We measure ourselves against others' job titles, salaries, promotions, and accomplishments. We scrutinize our looks, age, health, and even our romantic partners. We compare our lives with the airbrushed, luxury-filled, Technicolor posts of people on social media. We compare relationships, marriages, and families, too, creating a mental scoreboard that seems rigged against us.

When we buy into this illusion and believe that everyone around us is smarter, more attractive, more successful, happier, or wealthier, it's easy to get trapped in a cycle of self-doubt. But appearances can be deceiving. Comparison creates a misleading picture that everyone else has life figured out, which fuels feelings of inadequacy and dents confidence. Remember, what we see on the surface often reflects only the best, curated parts of others' lives, especially in today's world of well-polished, perfectly filtered social media highlights.

Thanks to my mom, I learned early on to embrace what makes me different. She encouraged me to focus on my own talents and goals.

"You'll never be happy if you're always comparing yourself to your twin sister Tracy," she said.

It's the same for all of us. We each have a unique skill set, talent, and purpose. Ever heard the saying: "Don't compare your chapter one with someone else's chapter twenty?" If you must compare yourself to someone, compare yourself with who you were 10 years ago, or even one year ago, and note the successes, achievements, progress, and growth that demonstrate how far you have come.

Fixating on the lives of others only serves as a distraction from your own goals. It detracts from your own potential. It blinds you to everything that makes you uniquely you. If you are constantly looking outward, you will always find someone "stronger," "smarter," "fitter," or "wealthier."

There's a powerful saying I live by: Comparison is the thief of joy. Measuring yourself against others can take away from your own happiness. It's a great reminder to focus inward and place your attention on your own qualities and strengths. Because that's what is going to make *you* a success. What makes you uniquely you? What makes you stand out from everyone else? Look for the contrasts, not the comparisons.

We're all guilty of trying to "keep up with the Joneses." Entrepreneurs often find themselves measuring their success against competitors. Artists may question the quality of their work compared with the quality of others. And every day, people scroll through highlight reels of others' lives, unaware of the struggles and setbacks that remain hidden off camera. This constant comparison creates a distorted reflection, like the carnival fun house mirror, warping our sense of reality and self-worth. Embracing our unique strengths and journey, rather than comparing ourselves to others, is key to appreciating our true potential. Einstein's words offer a vital reminder: "Everybody is a genius. But if you judge a fish by its ability to climb a tree, it will live its whole life believing that it is stupid."

3. The Face of Inadequacy

Do you ever feel like you're falling short and are "not good enough," no matter how much you accomplish? The feeling of inadequacy undermines confidence and likes to suggest that you lack what it takes to succeed: *I'm not good enough for this job. I'm not good enough to take on this project.* Or, in a relationship: *I'm not good enough for her/him.*

It's always a surprise to learn that the role models we revere also struggle with feeling inadequate. Famously, Michelle Obama revealed in her memoir *Becoming* that she's been plagued by the "Am I good enough?" question ever since her time as a student at Princeton. But she didn't let the doubt win. "I overcame that question the same way I do everything—with hard work. I decided to put my head down and let my work speak for itself. I had to get out of my own way."

That's the question we all have to ask: "How can I get out of my own way?"

At the root of it all, the not-good-enough belief is another example of the ego applying the brakes, not wanting your highest potential to be unleashed in case you fail. It would prefer to keep you in territory that's familiar and comfortable.

Every time misleading thoughts of inadequacy cross my mind, I don't listen to them. Because here's my attitude: How can you know if you're good enough at something unless you've actually tried?! There has to be a willingness to experiment with new things and new territory if you're going to go beyond your "limitations." It's the recognition that these limitations are self-imposed that can free you from the belief you are not enough.

I didn't know if I was good enough to run my own company, until I did.

I didn't know I could launch a product line, until I did.

There are a lot of people in the world who will sit on the sidelines, allowing themselves to be pushed aside by doubt. But I refuse to give doubt that power over me. As Michelle Obama says, get out of your own way, put your head down, and let your talents and qualities speak for you. If you're going to prove it to anyone, prove it to yourself.

From Self-Doubt to Self-Belief

Moving from self-doubt to self-belief involves cultivating trust in your own abilities and recognizing your inherent worth. With patience and consistent effort, you'll gradually empower yourself to pursue your goals with confidence. Here are four ways that I've flipped the script from self-doubt to self-belief:

1. Adopt the "Yes" Mindset

After realizing I had self-rejected the chance to sit on the corporate board, I kept the promise I made to myself: I said "yes" to every growth opportunity that came my way, regardless of how underqualified I felt.

In 2017, I can still remember being flooded with feelings of intimidation and pressure at being invited to speak to a group of 2,000 people at a *Success* magazine conference. The honor of the opportunity didn't make the prospect of speaking to that many people any less nerve-racking. Back then, my public speaking experience was limited to my own team or small groups of entrepreneurs—nothing compared with the size of this audience. The stakes felt even higher knowing I'd be sharing the stage with industry icons like Mel Robbins and

Brendon Burchard. Inevitably, the doubt started to creep in: *Am I really equipped to do this? Should I just politely decline?* But then I remembered my commitment to myself. So I accepted the invitation.

I countered the doubt by constantly rehearsing and practicing—preparation is an amazing antidote. While my fear didn't disappear altogether, it was definitely neutralized. When I finally took the stage at that sold-out venue, the feeling was electric. Yes, I still felt nervous, but I felt ready to take on the challenge! I stepped onto the stage and delivered my speech with confidence.

When I finished, my heart was still racing but I felt an over-whelming sense of pride. Not only for giving a successful speech but also for proving to *myself* that I'm capable of far more than my doubts would have me believe.

By understanding and learning to manage the faces of doubt, you make room for more opportunities because you're removing a huge psychological obstacle.

Next time you're invited to step into the spotlight, take on a new opportunity, or break from the usual, push past your doubt and just say "yes." Remind yourself of all the ways it will help you grow. Developing the habit of "yes" means you are actively cultivating the conditions for success. It forces you to consider all the reasons why *you can do something* rather than why you can't. And trust me, you are more capable than you realize.

The more times you say "yes," the more confidence you will build, and the more you will weaken the hold that self-doubt has over you. Say "yes" to learning as you go, and prove to yourself that growth and readiness come through experience, not just preparation.

Remember, every expert starts as a beginner. New attorneys don't gain real-life experience until handling their first trial. New pilots can't conquer the skies until they learn to fly and land the plane on their own. And new teachers can't truly grasp the role until they've faced a classroom during that first week of school. We all have to start somewhere. And our first step toward starting is to say "yes."

2. Be Your Own Coach

My youngest twin boys are absolutely crazy about soccer. They live and breathe the game, and every spare moment they're begging to watch their favorite players, Lionel Messi and Cristiano Ronaldo. One evening, we pulled up a Ronaldo highlights reel on YouTube, and they watched with wide-eyed admiration, barely blinking as he showcased his skills.

But then something unexpected happened. Ronaldo lined up to take a penalty as the whole stadium (and my boys) held their breath. But he didn't rush. He took a moment to close his eyes, then whispered to himself as he focused. And, according to the on-screen subtitles, he was telling himself, over and over, "You can do this!" and "It's normal for you to score!"

In that moment, Ronaldo's self–pep talk showed something beyond talent or skill. Even one of the greatest athletes in the world needed those words, those small reminders, to tune out the pressure and trust their ability. For my boys, it was a reminder that even their hero listens to his own words to quiet any doubts and to bring out his best when it matters most.

You, too, can do what Ronaldo did: Use self-encouragement to give yourself a pep talk. Be your own motivational coach. Remind yourself of all your strengths and how you have been in the same position before and succeeded.

Your voice of doubt can easily be replaced with your voice of belief.

Arianna Huffington, co-founder of *The Huffington Post* and Thrive Global, has her own way of combating self-doubt: "The greatest obstacle for me has been the voice in my head that I call my obnoxious roommate," she says. "I wish someone would invent a tape recorder that we could attach to our brains to record everything we tell ourselves. We would realize how important it is to stop this negative self-talk. It means pushing back against our obnoxious roommate with a dose of wisdom."

Lady Gaga has openly talked about her self-doubt, too, admitting to still feeling "like a loser kid in high school" despite tremendous success. In her documentary, she said she combats the doubt by telling herself every morning "that I'm a superstar, so that I can get through the day."

Whatever you choose to tell yourself, tell yourself only uplifting things rooted in fact. Echo your capabilities. Make it a daily practice to say you will succeed and you deserve to be where you are. The more often you start your day with such uplifting reminders, the more you will feel a mindset shift. Successful people believe they will succeed; they might experience thoughts of inadequacy, but they summon self-belief as a more powerful counterforce. They refuse to let doubt win. Ultimately, you become what you believe. And if you believe in yourself, the people around you will, too.

3. Achieve One Small Victory

Setting achievable goals is a powerful way to overcome self-doubt. When we aim for big goals or major accomplishments, it's easy to feel overwhelmed or uncertain about the scale of what lies ahead. But breaking down these goals into smaller, manageable steps provides a clear path forward and offers the chance to celebrate minor wins along the way.

After years of drowning in ambitious to-do lists, I discovered the transformative power of the "one small victory" approach. Every morning, before my inbox starts screaming for attention, I identify the single most important task that will move my life forward. Not 10 goals. Not five. One. It's simple but revolutionary. I shut down distractions, silence notifications, and drive all my energy toward that single victory. When I achieve it—whether it's finishing a crucial presentation or having that difficult conversation I've been avoiding—my confidence grows.

Each small victory becomes a brick in the foundation of larger confidence, and this daily practice prepares me to tackle larger challenges with unwavering belief in my ability to succeed. In the book *Atomic Habits*, James Clear emphasizes that small, consistent improvements can lead to long-term progress—this is the 1% principle. "Habits are the compound interest of self-improvement. Getting 1% better every day counts for a lot in the long-run." Small victory by small victory, you build the confidence to take on your biggest goals.

4. Visualize Success

This famous University of Chicago experiment proves that our minds can't always tell the difference between what we visualize and what we actually do. Picture this: Three groups of basketball players step onto a court.

One group practices free throws for a month.

The second group *only* visualizes taking perfect shots.

And the third group does nothing at all.

When they return to the court weeks later, something extraordinary happens: The players who only imagined making baskets improved nearly as much as those who physically practiced. It turns out that just *visualizing* the basketball soaring through the air and swishing into the net works wonders.[29]

Think of visualization as intentional daydreaming—using your imagination to create a clear mental picture of a successful outcome for any goal, project, or opportunity.

Take Michael Phelps, for example. In the run-up to a championship swim race, he didn't just train his body, he trained his mind. He mentally rehearsed the race by closing his eyes and picturing the setting, the pool, every stroke, every turn, and ultimately, his moment of victory. "He sees himself winning," Phelps's Olympic coach Bob Bowman told *Forbes* in 2016. "He smells the air, tastes the water, hears the sounds, sees the clock."

Phelps visualized his success, and you can do the same. Simply find somewhere to relax, then close your eyes and start imagining the successful outcome unfolding in real life. Play it out vividly in your mind—what it feels like, how you react, and what it signifies. If it can work for athletes, it can work for you. I use this visualization before big business pitches. I visualize the conversation, the energy, and the outcome I want. By picturing my success in advance, I feel more prepared and confident.

Every year, I create a "vision board" filled with magazine cutouts that reflect my dreams for the year ahead—my book on a bestseller list, a family vacation in Iceland, getting my beverage JUNI into Costco. I hang the board in my office so I can be reminded of my goals each day.

I believe so deeply in the power of vision boards that every December, I throw a vision board party. It's a tradition that turns goal setting into a full-blown celebration. My kitchen transforms into a creative lab—magazines, newspapers, and scraps of paper scattered everywhere, ready to be cut, pasted, and turned into mosaics of possibility. My friends and I spend hours hunting for images that capture everything from our career aspirations to personal dreams—creating physical blueprints of our future selves. What makes this ritual powerful isn't just the crafting; it's the way evocative visuals have the ability to bypass our logical brain and tap directly into our emotional core.

Research backs this up: People who commit their goals to paper are 33–42% more likely to achieve their goals compared to people who don't.[30] Dr. Gail Matthews's study highlights how writing down your goals can be a powerful catalyst for success.

When you see a vivid image of what you want, it imprints itself in your subconscious, helping you clarify your intentions and connect with your goals on a deeper level. I discovered this myself when a random photo of a Miami sunrise unexpectedly sparked my move across the country.

When I mention vision-boarding to friends or colleagues, I'm often met with skepticism. But the people who are so ready to dismiss visual anchors as pointless or simplistic don't know the transformative power of visualizing your future.

Take my friend Tom, the quintessential CEO—an Ivy League MBA with 15 years of experience leading Fortune 500 companies, known for his data-driven decision-making. When he unexpectedly lost his role at a major tech firm, his sense of identity was shaken to its core. "I've always been the guy with the plan," he told me over lunch. "For the first time in my career, I can't see the next step."

I suggested something that immediately made Tom—a man who had no patience for inspirational quotes—roll his eyes: Create a vision board. As I explained, "A vision board helps you see possibilities you didn't even know you were searching for."

"I'll think about it," he said, which I took as a "no."

Weeks later, Tom admitted that he finally gave it a try. As he pieced together images for his vision board—of camping trips, AI, self-driving cars—he started considering new possibilities. And it worked. Three months later, he launched a consulting firm focused on AI. "The vision board didn't create opportunities," he said. "but it opened my mind to recognize them."

The power of a vision board isn't in the pictures—it's in the mindset shift of possibility. As Tom can attest, sometimes the most powerful business tools aren't found in a spreadsheet but in the willingness to try something new. Have you ever tried creating a vision board? If not, you're missing out on a fun and inspiring way to bring your dreams to life. Ready to give it a go? Grab my free vision board guide at www .KimPerell.com/Resources and start crafting your vision today!

Believe In Yourself

It took me years to realize that success is about embracing who you are and trusting that it's more than enough. Too many times, I second-guessed my abilities and let uncertainty creep in. The mistake of believing I was underqualified wasn't just about missing opportunities; it was about a mindset that kept me small and reinforced my insecurities. It took years to recognize that my unique skills and experiences were assets, not liabilities, and that moments of doubt were simply challenges to grow stronger in my self-belief.

Think about every time you've done something great in your life. Were you really, truly ready? Or did you figure it out as you went along? That project you crushed, that pitch you nailed, that team you inspired, that proposal everyone loved—you weren't ready for any of it until you did it. That's not a coincidence—it's proof that growth happens in doing. So:

Apply for the job you feel underqualified for.

Say "yes" to the opportunity, ready or not.

Advocate for the raise you know you deserve.

Take a seat at the table where you're not an expert.

And in the face of doubt, remind yourself that you're way more qualified than you give yourself credit for. The only thing standing between you and the success you're meant for is believing it.

LESSON IN THE MISTAKE

The gap between where you are and where you want to be isn't filled with skills and qualifications—it's filled with belief.

CHAPTER SUMMARY

Self-reflection: When did you pass up an opportunity because you felt underqualified? Do you ever hold back your thoughts even when you have something valuable to contribute? How does feeling inadequate show up in your life?

Key Takeaways:

▶ **Self-Doubt Is Universal:** Everyone faces self-doubt at some point in their life. It is a natural response when you step outside your comfort zone, but it's a limiting thought, not a truth about your talents or potential.

▶ **Don't Self-Reject:** When you turn down opportunities simply because you think you're underqualified or inexperienced, you are limiting your potential. Be your own coach. Remind yourself what you CAN do.

▶ **Adopt the "Yes" Mindset:** Instead of finding reasons to doubt yourself, start the practice of saying "yes" to new opportunities, even when you feel underqualified. It is an empowering way to get into the habit of overcoming self-doubt.

▶ **Visualize Success:** Create a vision board to help you clarify your goals, stay motivated, and activate your brain's potential to recognize opportunities and turn your dreams into reality. Grab my vision board guide at www.KimPerell.com/Resources.

▶ **Challenge Self-Doubt with Action:** Every time you take action, despite feeling unsure, despite a sense of inadequacy, you diminish your doubt and reinforce your confidence.

▶ **Your Success, Your Terms:** Don't waste time by finding comparisons with others; find what sets you apart. Embrace what makes you unique.

Millionaire Mindset: I am worthy of the success that comes my way. It's why I say "yes" to new opportunities, regardless of self-doubt. My experience, skills, and perspective make me qualified to do new things that scare me. Each challenge I embrace builds confidence and self-belief.

Quitting Too Soon

Quitting can feel like the only escape when the weight of setbacks becomes unbearable. My mistake was thinking that quitting was the easiest way out.

I wish I could start this chapter with a dramatic story about how I quit something too soon and missed out on millions. You know the kind: "I was employee number four at Amazon but left because I thought online shopping was just a fad." But, the reality is: I've never actually made the mistake of quitting too soon.

And that's precisely why I'm uniquely qualified to write this chapter.

I've gotten *so* close to quitting more times than I can count. I've drafted the resignation emails. I've practiced the "I quit" speech in the mirror. I've had the "maybe I should just shut it down" thought at 3 AM. I know intimately the psychology of what drives us to that edge, because I've stood on it repeatedly. In fact, the ledge and I are good friends!

But here's what makes my perspective valuable even though I've never actually quit too soon: I've discovered something fascinating about the moment right before someone reaches their breaking point.

That's the moment of truth—the psychological inflection point where everything within you screams "QUIT!" But that urge is actually a test. A test that most people fail because they don't recognize it for what it is: your brain's last-ditch effort to protect you from the discomfort of pushing through.

Think of me as your field researcher who's been to the edge, documented the experience, and come back with the data on why that moment is so deceptive. I've practically developed a scientific understanding of the difference between when quitting feels right (which is often) and when it actually *is* right (rarely).

The irony isn't lost on me that one of my biggest "mistakes" around quitting is that I don't do it. But that stubbornness has given me a front-row seat to what happens when you push beyond the quitting point. And let me tell you, that's exactly where the magic usually happens.

Every millionaire faces a moment when quitting seems like the only (and easiest) option. A crushing setback, a devastating blow, a massive financial loss that makes you question everything—these are the times when the temptation to quit is strongest. *I'm exhausted . . . I've had enough . . . I can't do this anymore . . . I might as well quit.* We've all been there. Your lowest point is your weakest point. But know this: Each setback will only make you smarter, sharper, and stronger. After experiencing countless setbacks, I've learned that the exact moment you want to walk away is the same moment you might be a few steps away from massive success.

When I'm asked in interviews or on podcasts, about the qualities I like to see in aspiring entrepreneurs, the answer is easy: perseverance. It's a "warrior spirit"—an invaluable trait that runs like a golden thread through every millionaire I know.

Those who succeed are not people who never fail; they are people who never quit.

Because if you quit too soon, you will never know the possibilities that lie ahead or what might have been.

Ronald Wayne co-founded Apple with Steve Jobs and Steve Wozniak in 1976 but sold his 10% stake back to them after just 12 days, making $800. Had he kept his equity, those shares would be worth more than $100 billion today.[31]

Stephen King, when writing his debut novel, *Carrie*, threw away the first few pages and gave up on the book entirely. In his mind it was a failure; clumsy and artless. Thankfully, his wife rescued those pages from the trash and encouraged him to continue writing the story.[32] If she hadn't, Stephen might never have published the worldwide best-seller that established him as a new voice in American fiction.

King's early struggles exemplify a universal truth about bringing dreams to life—something my grandfather often reminded me: "Kim, everything takes twice as long, costs twice as much, and takes twice as much energy as you anticipate. Assume there will be complications, delays, rejection, chaos. Expect it all."

With a millionaire mindset, you face adversity head-on. It's about not overreacting; it's about keeping a cool, calm head when everyone else might be losing theirs. If you stay clear on your vision, approach crises constructively, and focus on solutions over problems, you can handle most challenges.

————

When I was 16, my dad gave me *Think and Grow Rich* by Napoleon Hill, which is still one of my favorite books today. It contains a powerful story of quitting too soon.

The story follows a determined gold miner who invests in mining equipment and sets out to strike gold. For weeks, he drills tirelessly from sunrise to sundown, believing success is just within reach. But as time goes on, his confidence begins to wane and doubt creeps in. Exhausted and discouraged, he finally decides to quit.

The miner sells his equipment to a local junkman, assuming it's worthless. But instead of giving up, the junkman does something different—he seeks advice from a mining expert. The expert tells the junkman that a massive gold vein still exists in those hills. Armed with this new knowledge, the junkman picks up in the same spot where the original miner quit. And with just a little more digging, he strikes gold, landing himself a life-changing fortune . . . just three feet away from the spot where the original miner had quit. It's a story that reminds us that success may be just around the corner. Even when we're on the verge of giving up, we may be just "three feet from gold."

The lesson is clear: When you've worked so hard and come so far, why would you quit so easily? Whatever your pursuit, it's a sense of discipline and commitment that will push you across the finish line. Of course, not all plans work out. There are true dead ends and unrecoverable situations that we have to accept. But I never give up on something I'm committed to, until I've exhausted every conceivable solution.

Throughout my career, I've found myself revisiting Napoleon Hill's "three feet from gold" story time and again, most recently with one of my newest companies, Cay Skin. I've always believed in pushing forward, no matter how tough things get. But launching Cay Skin tested that belief in ways I never could have imagined—because if there was ever a moment I almost walked away, this was it.

———————

In late spring of 2020, I was focused on finding innovative ideas to incubate under my holding company, 100.co. I'd already invested in JUNI, and many pitches came across my desk, but nothing else had piqued my interest. Until the day I met supermodel Winnie Harlow.

Winnie had a bold vision for a sunscreen product and needed a business partner to help bring it to life. I first learned about Winnie when she was a contestant on *America's Next Top Model* in 2014, marking the first time that a model with the autoimmune skin condition vitiligo was showcased on a global stage. Her striking appearance quickly made her one of the most recognizable faces in the world. Michael Jackson had the same condition but went to great lengths to cover it up, whereas Winnie embraced it. "It's a part of me but it doesn't define me," she said.

Since then, she's appeared on the covers of *Vogue*, *Elle*, and *Marie Claire*, and served as a judge on *Project Runway*; she has starred in music videos for Beyoncé, Shakira, and Calvin Harris; she has walked the runway for Victoria's Secret, Fendi, and Marc Jacobs; and she has been the face of Puma and Tiffany & Co.

What perhaps isn't conveyed by her high-fashion glossy photos is the warmth and authenticity that immediately struck me when we first met in Santa Monica, soon after the city had reopened post–Covid lockdown. At our three-hour lunch, it was her perseverance that impressed me the most.

In sharing some of her childhood struggles, Winnie explained how she was bullied by kids who called her "zebra" and "cow" because of her vitiligo. Those comments hit Winnie hard, but from her pain emerged an extraordinary strength . . . and an unbreakable spirit.

When she pitched her business idea to me, she explained how vitiligo makes her especially prone to sunburn, and how finding a sunscreen that didn't leave a white cast on her skin was impossible. For a supermodel, that was a *huge* problem. Outdoor photo shoots became challenging because the sunscreen's white residue looked purplish in photos. One particular shoot in the Bahamas in 2018 made her realize she *had* to take action.

For two days, she worked from sunrise to sunset in the punishing sun. The sunscreen she had applied in the morning left the unsightly white cast and to ensure the pictures looked perfect, she stopped reapplying protection. "I compromised protecting my skin for looking beautiful . . . and burned to a crisp," she said.

Her sunburn was so severe that she needed medical treatment.

As she reflected on that photo shoot, she realized that sunscreen wasn't just a beauty choice, it was a health necessity.

As she told me over lunch: "The importance of protecting your skin shouldn't be compromised because it *doesn't look good*. I want to create a sunscreen that works for every skin tone—without the white cast."

I was all ears, intrigued by her bold vision.

"No one has done it before," she added. "Creating a universal sunscreen for every race would be a world first."

Winnie's mission resonated on a deeply personal level for me because skin cancer runs in my family. I've had multiple diagnoses of basal cell cancer myself, making me extremely conscious of sun exposure. It's also made me hyperaware of the stats: one in five people will develop skin cancer in their lifetime, according to the American Academy of Dermatology.[33]

I left the restaurant feeling energized by her idea of creating a product that could not only protect but potentially save lives. By the next morning, my mind was made up. I called Winnie first thing. "You've got your co-founder and investor. Let's make this happen!"

We had all the ingredients for success: purpose, influence, and an industry ripe for disruption. Winnie, the most famous Black supermodel of her generation, had a platform of 10 million followers who valued her perspective—positioning her as the ideal person to bring this much-needed sunscreen to market.

Ultimately, we landed on the brand name Cay Skin. (Cay—inspired by Winnie's Jamaican roots—refers to small islands in the

Caribbean). Finding a name turned out to be the easy part. Creating the actual sunscreen proved to be more challenging.

Being new to the industry, I didn't realize how hard it would be, but I quickly came to understand why there might be a reason that creating a sunscreen for all skin types had never been done before. Even industry giants hadn't cracked the elusive formula.

We were determined to get it right.

The following months were all trial and error: sampling, smelling, and scrutinizing different formulas. Winnie was both our guinea pig and toughest customer. If a test sunscreen left even the slightest residue, we went back to the drawing board. Over and over and again.

Eventually, we landed on a formula that also reflected Winnie's Jamaican heritage: island-based ingredients such as aloe, nectar, and sea moss. Our magic ingredient was rutin—a natural yellow mineral that helps mitigate the white cast often associated with sunscreens. We were thrilled to see that it worked perfectly when tested across all skin tones. It was the final confirmation we needed, and we were ready to take it to market.

Our first major win came in the spring of 2021 when we secured a pitch meeting with Sephora. With their commitment to beauty innovation and support for Black-owned brands, they were the ideal partner. Due to the pandemic, the meeting had to be held via Zoom, but that didn't impact the effectiveness of the pitch. Winnie didn't just tell her story—she proved it firsthand. "I won't just tell you how our product is different from anything out there," she said. "I'll show you."

First, she applied a standard sunscreen to her forearm, leaving a white residue on her skin. Then, she used Cay—this time, no white cast. Our fast-absorbing sunscreen blended seamlessly into every shade of her skin. "And this is the problem we're solving," said Winnie, her skin radiant and residue free.

Sephora's executives couldn't ignore the contrast between our product and the generic. "We'd like to offer you an opportunity to launch Cay Skin sunscreen products in 250 stores," said the head buyer.

In our wildest dreams, we couldn't have imagined we'd get the opportunity to launch on such a large scale right from the start. Typically, brands spend years proving themselves, building traction and demonstrating demand before a retailer will consider giving them shelf space. But with Sephora's support, we were able to launch both in store and online from day one. A rare opportunity that most founders dream of.

From that point on, momentum picked up quickly. We raised $4 million in funding, which made Winnie one of only 100 Black female founders to ever raise over $1 million. Every piece of the puzzle was falling into place, and it truly felt like we were making history!

Our first product photo shoot exceeded all our expectations. Picture Winnie standing in the crystal-clear blue waters of Miami Beach, wearing a gorgeous white bathing suit, proudly holding the bottle of sunscreen she'd once dreamed about creating. Surrounded by models, in sleek white suits, they laughed and splashed in the water. The whole day couldn't have gone more smoothly.

When the photographer shouted, "That's a wrap!" everyone cheered.

As we packed up, we heard some murmurings among the crew: Apparently a wardrobe stylist had noticed some yellow stains on the white bathing suits.

Yellow stains . . . ?

In the euphoria of the moment, with the perfect photos captured, we brushed off what seemed like a minor issue.

And that would prove to be a HUGE mistake . . .

———

We all know Murphy's Law: Anything that can go wrong will go wrong. Well, I also have a law, but Kim's Law goes a little differently—it says that anything that can go wrong will go wrong, worse than you thought, and at the worst possible time. And the entire Cay Skin story is the perfect demonstration of Kim's Law in action.

We officially launched as a brand in March 2022 with the kind of fanfare you would expect when a beloved supermodel launches a beauty line. We went to market with six products: two universal mineral sunscreens, three face and body lotions, and an SPF lip balm. As Cay Skin launched in Sephora stores and online, we received incredible media coverage, from *People, Elle,* and *Cosmopolitan* magazines to *Forbes, USA Today,* and *The Daily Mail.* We couldn't have imagined a stronger launch—and things kept getting better.

In the world of startups, the most fulfilling moments come when your vision transforms into reality right before your eyes. For us, that moment came when Winnie and I first stepped into a Sephora in Los Angeles and saw our product glimmering on the shelf of the "Next Big Thing" wall—a dedicated section showcasing innovative beauty brands. As customers lined up for selfies with Winnie, I felt a surge of pride. This wasn't just a product launch; it was the physical manifestation of Winnie's vision and perseverance.

Later that week, I was in the middle of my quarterly board meeting for 100.co when my cell vibrated with a text from the Cay Skin CEO: "Kim, can you talk?"

You know it's something bad when someone asks you that question. When she picked up, her voice was shaking. "We've got a big problem. Our sunscreen is making people's skin look yellow!"

Wait. What? Yellow?

"Our customer service team is getting inundated with complaints from social media," she said.

I was in disbelief, but more than anything, confused.

She emailed me a dozen complaints, and, as I read the different grievances my stomach sank.

"I look like the sun!"

"I wore this to a dance class, and halfway through the class I looked in the mirror and saw my face dripping with YELLOW . . ."

"My white top is stained yellow! Are you gonna pay for my laundry?"

These first complaints turned out to be the early, faint drumbeat of a growing crisis. Over the following days, that drumbeat grew louder with each new batch of unhappy customers. And then it reached a peak with a disparaging video review of our mineral sunscreen by a beauty YouTuber who had millions of followers.

With a sense of panic rising, I pressed Play and watched the YouTube influencer tear apart our product in real time. It was a scathing, scorched-earth review. Snippets of that commentary still haunt me: "It's turning me yellow . . . I can't go out like this . . . Life is too short to use a crappy sunscreen!"

If you can trust one thing about scathing reviews, it's their ability to go viral . . . and this one was watched over a million times. I closed my laptop and sat there paralyzed by shock. I couldn't fathom how quickly our dream launch had turned into a nightmare.

The impact was devastating—financially, emotionally, and culturally. We had no choice but to pull our two mineral sunscreens off Sephora's shelves. Our other sunscreen products remained in stores, but that didn't soften the blow of a very public humiliation. In an instant, all our hard work and millions of dollars invested were at risk.

It was such an avoidable mistake, too. How could something like this slip by?! I wasn't involved in the day-to-day operations and I needed answers. But those answers would have to wait. The immediate concern was whether our company could even come back from this disaster.

I picked up the phone and called Winnie, and could hear the sound of defeat in her voice. She was, after all, the face of the brand. But, as we brainstormed how to fix the problem, I once again saw her perseverance that had stood out to me during our first lunch.

"I grew up in the hood, Kim," she said. "Hardship and setbacks aren't new to me. Life has taught me that every challenge holds a lesson. We'll learn from this and come back even stronger."

I've encountered many crushing setbacks in business, and the only way failure becomes final is if *you choose* to quit. Winnie and I shared the same resolve—no setback could diminish the spirit of our brand or what Cay Skin stood for.

The first thing we needed to do was carry out a postmortem and identify what part of the formulation was causing people to turn yellow. The team debrief was strained, to say the least. Everyone felt embarrassed, and there were a lot of pointing fingers.

"Didn't we test the product?"

"I thought you were responsible for—"

"How did you let this happen?"

Everyone was focused on diverting blame, an indication that the situation had deteriorated to the point where the entire team was on the defensive.

Ultimately, we found the cause of the issue: It turned out that the rutin levels were accidentally increased before production, causing the yellowing of the product to stain faces and clothes. The conversation focused on "should haves." We *should have* had more controls in place. Our testing *should have* been tighter. But rather than wasting time pointing fingers, I focused on bringing the team together.

"It's our mistake to own," I said. "It's also our problem to fix. If we work together, we'll make it right."

But despite my best efforts to turn the tide, team morale had bottomed out. It felt like a row of falling dominoes—first, our head of product development resigned, then our head of marketing. What was once a tight-knit team was slowly unraveling at the edges.

The go-forward plan was to rehire key roles, fix the formula, and eventually relaunch the product. The sunscreen market thrives from February to August, and if you miss that "sun season" window, you miss out on crucial sales. So the pressure was on. If we didn't get our sunscreen back on the shelves in time for that window, the future of Cay would be in jeopardy. We had 10 months to turn things around.

Despite this setback, our other existing products earned rave reviews, and Sephora offered to expand Cay into 100 stores in Canada. This was a huge win but also required more money—*a lot* more. Without a substantial influx of cash, there was no way we would pull it off. With the clock ticking, Winnie and I decided to invest our own money, which underscored our commitment *and* resonated with our existing investors who followed suit. A great reminder that to ignite belief in others, you first have to bet on yourself.

Launching in another country demands a tremendous amount of time, energy, and logistical effort. It took us months of navigating complex legal requirements to get our product approved for sale in Canada.

———————

In April 2023, Cay Skin launched in Canada, in Winnie's hometown of Ontario. It felt like the perfect launchpad, going back to her roots. We had a huge press tour in place—back-to-back TV interviews, features lined up with fashion magazines, and an in-store meet and greet. In the days leading up to the event, we were told that thousands of people were going to be at Sephora to see Winnie's "homecoming." It promised to be a monumental moment for the brand.

And then, two days before launch, my phone rang.

It was Winnie and our CEO. "Kim, can you talk? We've got a problem . . ."

Not again. What now?!

Canadian customs had decided to hold our product for an "undetermined amount of time." I couldn't believe our terrible luck. It meant we had no product for the store launch, the media tour, or the fans coming to support Winnie. And we had no idea if the product would clear customs in two days, two weeks, or two months. The only Cay Skin products in Canada were in Winnie's purse—an almost-empty bottle of face sunscreen and one half-used lip balm.

"What are we going to do?" asked Winnie. "Should we postpone the launch?"

I could hear the exhaustion in our CEO's voice, mirroring my own. Neither of us had a perfect answer. Reaching this point had been utterly draining. We were stretched thin, and it seemed like no matter how hard we tried, we couldn't catch a break.

I had to step away for a minute to gather my thoughts. I often have to remind myself to do this in a crisis. To breathe. To regain a sense of perspective. Because, in the heat of this moment, it felt like I was at my limit.

I called my husband John at home. I'm not sure he's ever heard me sound so exasperated. Was it time to give up? We talked about the possibility of postponing the launch, but I also knew I needed to take off my emotion-colored lenses and look at the situation pragmatically.

No smart decision is ever made when emotions are running high.

After the call, I put my phone in a drawer and took a long walk. I switched off—not easy for me to do! After a few hours, though still emotional, I felt more confident in my ability to be objective.

Winnie and I carefully considered our two options: Launch the product without anything to sell, or postpone. For me, there was only one choice: Make the best of a bad situation and let the show go on.

"It's not ideal," I told Winnie, "but if anyone can pull off a press tour without a product, it's you!"

Without missing a beat, she said, "Let's do it!"

Sure enough, Winnie flawlessly navigated TV interviews and a high-profile press lunch, and she dazzled her fans at the in-store launch. Thankfully customers appreciated our candor and were understanding. We created enough of a buzz to sustain interest until customs released our product (which happened a couple of weeks later).

When we stepped back and saw all the glowing media coverage, the lack of product seemed almost inconsequential. Even better, summer sales continued to skyrocket, and Sephora responded by offering to expand the brand from 250 stores to 550 stores. We were elated!

———————

Despite our success, the headwinds facing us remained strong. In order to expand, we needed to raise more money to buy extra inventory. But with the challenging economic climate, fundraising had dried up, and it was harder than ever to raise capital. As weeks turned into months, the company's bank account kept shrinking, and we still hadn't found new investors.

The stress became unbearable and proved too much for our CEO, who had been in the trenches with us. She finally hit her breaking point and gave two weeks' notice. Honestly, with the way things were going, I didn't blame her for resigning. In the back of my mind, all I could think was: *How far are we from gold? Three feet? Twelve feet? . . . Two miles?*

After a particularly rough day of investor rejections, I drove home feeling overwhelmed by a sense of hopelessness. There was no way we were going to survive without a CEO and investment.

I walked into my house, dropped my bag, and collapsed onto the couch. John took one look at me. "How much longer are you going to do this?"

I didn't even hesitate. "I'm done. I quit."

It felt definitive. It felt right. It felt like the only rational thing to do. There was no way I could save the company. I asked the CEO to spend her final two weeks drafting a plan to wind down the company.

During that time, I lived as if I had quit. I told friends I was shutting down the company. I stopped stress-checking my email at midnight. I mentally moved on.

Yet still, something gnawed at me. *Wait . . . am I actually quitting? Is this really it?*

I'd wake up every morning sure of my choice: *Yes. I quit. Move on!*

By dinner? *Okay . . . but am I quitting too soon?*

This continued for 14 consecutive nights—I mentally quit every morning and then unquit every evening.

Until, I finally acknowledged reality: If I had really quit, why was I still obsessing over it?

It was belief. Belief in what we were doing and the difference Cay was going to make. The same belief that had sustained us through yellow-tinted customers and products trapped in Canadian customs. This is the paradox of entrepreneurship: Sometimes, the greatest moments of doubt are also your moments of deepest conviction.

So, instead of quitting, I doubled down and took on the role of interim CEO. I didn't have the time, but, once again, it was better than quitting. I found myself as the CEO of JUNI and Cay Skin, juggling responsibilities while trying to keep everything on track at two very different companies. The first thing I did was assess Cay's current state. I needed to know exactly where we stood—what was working, what wasn't working, and how much time we had before we ran out of money entirely.

The answer was sobering. If we were going to survive, we needed a serious cash injection. And there were no investors in sight. That left only one option: If I believed in this company, I had to prove it. I ran the numbers, debated the risks, and played out the worst-case scenarios. Then, I made the call. I invested another million dollars.

Belief isn't just what you tell yourself when things get hard. It's what you're prepared to bet on—when no one else will.

This was an investment in the possibility of what Cay could become. With that decision, exhaustion gave way to a fresh burst of determination.

While my million dollars provided the capital to cover operating costs, we still needed double that amount to purchase inventory to expand into 550 stores the following year. So, the pursuit for new investors continued.

Winnie and I took meetings with more than 100 VC firms, in San Francisco, New York, and Miami. We even flew to Paris to pitch a huge beauty investor. We faced rejection after rejection, running into the same brick wall. "You're too early . . . Come back to us when you have more traction." We continued to hear "no" after "no" after "no" . . . and watched our bank account steadily shrink.

But we never lost hope because we never lost sight of the harsh reality that comes with entrepreneurship: You'll face many closed doors before knocking on one that opens. If you're not prepared for rejection, you will never be a millionaire.

Winnie and I knew we needed to keep going until we found investors who believed in our vision for Cay. We kept reminding each other that the more investors we spoke to, the more our odds improved. And just as our self-reassurances started to sound hollow, and after months of more meetings and dead ends, our luck turned.

Feeling weary but putting on brave faces, we walked into an afternoon meeting with potential investors at the Beverly Hills Hotel. To our pleasant surprise, they displayed genuine interest. Instead of a "no," we got a "let's talk further." Those talks led to three months of due diligence, and that's when we received the lifeline we'd been waiting for—they decided to invest, on the condition they would bring in their own CEO and support team. This was the best-case scenario, having experienced beauty executives step in to take over my role as CEO and manage the company's operations. For the first time in a long time, we had the support we desperately needed.

With fresh funding and a new team filled with optimism, we reformulated, repackaged, and relaunched our mineral sunscreen . . . and, this time, it didn't turn anyone yellow. More importantly, it *sold out* and earned rave reviews online. The product we'd envisioned from the very beginning finally became a reality.

There were many moments when we weren't sure we'd even make it, let alone find investors who shared our vision. As with any startup, I know there will be more challenges ahead for Cay. But, no matter what happens next, I'll look back with no regrets—because we gave it everything we had.

Having founded nearly a dozen companies, I've learned that the ones that succeed don't quit when it gets tough. They persevere despite the urge to quit, always believing they're just three feet from gold.

The Three Quitting Triggers

In my experience, there are three common quitting triggers: the emotional quit, the rejection quit, and the bad-luck quit. I've faced all three, and I know how easily they can disguise themselves as justifications for giving up.

1. The Emotional Quit

Emotions drive human behavior. The decisions we make are dictated by how we feel at any given moment. When it comes to make-or-break decisions around giving up or going the distance, *stepping away* from your emotions is crucial.

Any kind of significant setback can be crushing, especially when you have invested heart and soul into a company, a creation, a project, or a relationship. But acting impulsively in the heat of emotion can lead to decisions you'll later regret. Avoiding an "emotional quit" requires discipline and mental clarity.

Take the example of my public brand crisis with Cay and the yellowing sunscreen disaster. The initial wave of emotions—hopelessness, sadness, anger—were overwhelming, but I knew better than to react impulsively. Instead, I stepped back to give myself distance and focus on activities that grounded me before making any critical decisions. This reset allowed me to recharge mentally and gain clarity.

If you don't have enough mental distance to be objective, here's a useful mindfulness technique:

1. Find a quiet place. Close your eyes.
2. Pay attention to your emotions. What are you feeling?
3. Simply observe them, without getting involved with them, as if you're watching each emotion pass by on a conveyor belt.
4. As they pass, label them. For example: "That's shame" or "That's anger" or "That's guilt"—and let them go by, focusing on the next emotion that comes into view.
5. Do this for five minutes, pointing out each emotion in your own mind until you feel calmer and clearer.

The point of this exercise is to honor your emotions, let them surface, then let them drift away, observing them as *something separate* from you. Instead of thinking *I am angry* or *I am stressed*, you think *That's anger* or *That's sadness*. You feel them; you don't become them. It's amazing how this little switch in perspective can make all the difference. So next time you encounter a crushing setback and feel the temptation to throw in the towel, use this technique to help you distinguish between emotional quitting and rational quitting.

2. The Rejection Quit

Every rejection I've experienced has felt personal and painful. In my early years in business, it left me hiding under the duvet, shutting out the world. But I've since learned to embrace rejection as a gift that pushes me to try harder and redirects me toward a new path.

The value of the many "noes" you accumulate on the way to success only becomes apparent when you receive the one "yes" that matters. Winnie and I could put a series of investor rejections into perspective only when we finally found the perfect investor.

Rejection, like failure, gets a bad rap because it's often framed as something in opposition to success. But rejection is actually an essential part of the journey to success!

Look at Michael Jordan—cut from his high school basketball team and told he wasn't good enough. Did he see rejection as a reflection of his talent? Not at all. He stuck with it and went on to win six NBA championships. When James Dyson set out to reinvent the vacuum cleaner, he created 5,126 prototypes that all failed. Finally, one succeeded, and he transformed the vacuum industry, achieving a personal net worth of $4.5 billion in the process. But what if he'd let rejection stop him?

And let's not forget J.K. Rowling. Her first manuscript was rejected *12 times* before she published *Harry Potter and the Philosopher's Stone* and sold 10 million copies. And then there's the inventor of Spanx, Sara Blakely, who desperately needed a prototype for her "footless pantyhose" idea, but every factory in North Carolina rejected her. Sarah kept cold-calling until one factory owner decided to back the "crazy idea" that made her a billionaire.

The next time you face rejection, see it as a gift—an opportunity to learn and adapt, rather than give up and quit.

3. The Bad-Luck Quit

In Cay's first year, I encountered a streak of terrible luck. Our continuous setbacks felt like a sign from the universe to give up.

With every setback, you must make a decision: Give up or get smarter; walk away or push harder. However hard you work, and despite your best intentions, curveballs will happen and test your resilience. The entrepreneurs who make it are the ones who keep pushing forward, led by an unwavering belief in their idea. One of my favorite quotes from Thomas Jefferson is: "I'm a great believer in luck, and I find the harder I work, the more I have of it."

The companies that survive and thrive in the face of bad luck are the ones that uncover opportunities hidden within crisis. They don't let setbacks define their path. So the next time you're hit with a stroke of bad luck, pause and reassess the situation. Don't see it as the end. See it as the beginning of your next breakthrough.

Know When It's Time to Quit

While it's important not to quit too soon, it's equally important to know when quitting is *the right thing to do*. Everybody's situation is going to be different, and each person will have their own limits, but quitting is sometimes the smartest thing to do. Deep down, I think we all know when we've pushed things as far as we can. At that point, it becomes a matter of courage. In a society that tends to label people as quitters or lazy or unambitious, recognizing when it's time to walk away takes a level of courage that matches the determination needed to keep going.

Perseverance should never mean pushing yourself to the point where a never-say-die attitude ends up hurting you, financially, emotionally, or physically. It is one thing to be positive and optimistic, showing grit and determination; it is another to wear rose-tinted glasses. So if you're wondering whether enough is enough, here are three surefire indicators that tell you it's time to consider walking away.

1. Financial Loss

You have to know when to cut your losses. If you're having trouble paying your bills, it's a clear sign that quitting might be the smartest thing to do. Remember, you started a business to make money, not lose it.

With my first company, all I had was the $10,000 from my Nanny and a credit card limit of $20,000—that was the maximum amount I was willing (and able) to lose. Setting a financial loss limit is crucial when starting a new venture. One thing that has helped me is to write down my financial loss limit and make a promise to myself not to exceed it. Have a concrete number as the red line you will not cross; that line will tell you when it's time to quit. Establishing limits stops you from making reckless choices in the heat of the moment.

2. Lack of Passion

Losing your passion or motivation indicates that your heart's not invested anymore. If you wake up dreading the day ahead, you need to step back and remind yourself *why* you started in the first place. Does your "why" still resonate? Does it energize and inspire you? If the answer is "no," then quitting becomes a serious option to consider. There are many reasons that you may have lost your mojo. Something else could be going on in your life that's stealing your focus and energy. Or you might have found a new passion you want to pursue. If you're not passionate about what you are doing, and you're not energized about the path you are on, it may be a sign that you should quit.

3. Your Health Is Suffering

Your mental and physical health are your foundation—everything else in your life depends on them. If you're feeling burned out, overwhelmed, or struggling to stay healthy, it's your body's way of sending you a message to live life differently. Early in my career, I was all about the grind—pulling all-nighters and running on fumes. It seemed to be the only way to succeed. But over time, I learned the hard way that pushing myself to the limit wasn't sustainable.

My mom's first job was as an occupational therapist at a large hospital working with patients recovering from strokes, heart attacks, and depression. She'd hear them say, "I don't have time for this—I need to get back to work." It's a situation many people face, but the truth is—if you don't have your health, you can't show up fully for your work. My mom's stories stuck with me, and as I watched friends and colleagues deal with serious health issues brought on by job-related stress, it hit even harder. That's when I made a promise to myself: My health comes first, no exceptions. If you make millions but can't enjoy it, what's the point? There's no shame in walking away from something that is harmful to your health.

Setbacks and challenges don't have to mark the end of your journey. Instead, they can be a test of how much you're willing to fight for what you want. As my Cay story shows, entrepreneurship is a wild roller-coaster ride—exhilarating highs one moment and exasperating lows the next. That's the nature of the beast. You'll feel every emotion, face character-testing challenges, and maybe even question your own sanity, but in those moments when everything seems to be going wrong, it's worth reminding yourself of what motivated you to start in the first place.

What was your original vision? What difference did you hope to make, in your life or the lives of others? If you can remind yourself of why you started, and if you can find reasons to keep going, you won't walk away because, deep down, you'll know there is still something worth fighting for.

Next time you're exhausted and ready to quit, ask yourself: What if I'm only three feet from gold?

LESSON <small>IN THE</small> MISTAKE

Success is not a straight
path—it's a winding road full
of detours, roadblocks, and
dead ends. Take a break, rest,
and recharge. Just don't quit.

CHAPTER SUMMARY

Self-reflection: Think about a time when you came close to quitting but didn't. What made you stay? What did you learn from that experience?

Key Takeaways:

▶ **"Three Feet from Gold":** When you feel like quitting, you might be closer to success or a breakthrough than you think. Always ask yourself: "Could I be three feet from gold? Is it worth persevering?"

▶ **Embody the Warrior Spirit:** Those who succeed are not people who never fail; they are people who never quit. Adopt the "warrior spirit"–expect complications, delays, rejection, and chaos . . . and take them in stride.

▶ **Rejection Is Redirection:** Rejection is part of the journey. Each "no" brings you closer to a "yes." Rejection is redirection to somewhere, someone, or something else.

▶ **Emotions Cloud Judgment:** No smart decisions are ever made when emotions are high. Acting on emotions can lead to irrational choices. Distance yourself from your feelings. Find calm and clarity before making any major decisions.

▶ **Use Effective Reset Techniques:** If you're tempted to quit, take at least 24 hours before making a decision. Use positive diversions such as exercise and meditation to reset, calm your mind, and reassess the situation.

▶ **Know When It's Time to Quit:** Sometimes the bravest and smartest thing IS recognizing it's time to quit, especially if you're experiencing financial loss, you've lost passion, or your health is suffering.

Millionaire Mindset: I face adversity and setbacks with the belief that everything will work out. I keep a cool, calm head because, whatever happens around me, I stay true to my vision, navigate a crisis in a constructive way, and focus on what I can control, not what I can't.

Thinking Business Isn't Personal

Success isn't about closing deals—it's about building relationships.
When I finally understood that, everything changed.

"It's not personal, it's strictly business."

These famous words from the movie *The Godfather* are heard not only in back alleys but in boardrooms, a camouflage used by Wall Street executives and Mafia dons alike. It's a familiar disguise. A smoke screen. A way to distance ourselves from the weight of a tough decision.

The idea that business isn't personal? That's a myth. Personal emotions and business decisions are deeply entwined, as interconnected as the roots of a tree. Every decision, every deal, every partnership—it all comes down to people. Whether you're closing a big deal, hiring your first employee, or giving feedback during a weekly check-in, there's always a personal impact.

I've been working long enough to know that some people truly do operate with a "strictly business" mindset, but every million-dollar deal I've ever closed came down to one thing: making it personal. And the one time I didn't understand that value, it almost ruined my career.

When I launched my first company, Frontline Direct, I was obsessed with optimizing every minute. As a solopreneur, I had convinced myself there wasn't time for the "personal" stuff. I treated client meetings like surgical procedures—get in, get out. That was how I operated, certain that being purely professional would disguise the fact that I was 23, a woman, and had never run a company. No time for coffee chats, no personal stories, and definitely no jokes. I naively thought business was just a simple exchange: The client pays for results, and I deliver them. End of story. Like a human vending machine—insert money, receive services. I was so focused on proving I was worth my clients' time that I forgot what actually makes people want to spend their time with you: personal connection.

Even though my business had been thriving, I started losing clients, and growth began to slow. My solution? Work even harder to keep the clients I still had. Pour more hours into producing better outcomes. At the time, "fixing things" meant doubling down on what I could control.

That same year, I had half a dozen clients who were going to CES, one of the largest technology trade shows, held annually in Las Vegas. Initially, I had no intention of going myself. From Hawaii, a cross-Pacific flight for a conference seemed like the definition of inefficiency. Plus, I was a one-stop shop. If I wasn't working, nothing was getting done. But then, my biggest client assumed I was attending and asked to meet at the conference, so I immediately booked my flight.

To my surprise, I found that I genuinely enjoyed being at CES. Meeting face-to-face with people I'd only connected with over phone or by email was incredibly energizing. Every conversation revealed nuances about their business that my perfectly crafted reports had missed. Being there felt like the opposite of a waste of time; it felt like a great investment of my time and energy—shaking hands, making connections, looking people in the eye, and understanding them on a level beyond just business.

On the last day of the conference, I carried this newfound energy into that meeting with my biggest client. But my smile quickly faded when I found out the reason he wanted to meet wasn't to talk through goals for the new year—he was ending our partnership.

"You did great work, Kim, but this is the first time you've taken the time to meet with us," he said. "We are evolving and need a partner that understands our short-term needs and our long-term strategy." I was completely taken aback.

Later that evening, I found myself at the airport lounge, trying to make sense of what had happened. My laptop was open in front of me, but I couldn't focus. I was gazing out the window, feeling defeated, when a stranger struck up a conversation with me.

"In town for the conference?" The man, in his sixties, wearing an elegant suit, gestured to the CES badge sticking out of my bag.

"Yes." I tried to muster a smile.

He pulled out his own badge from his briefcase. "You know, this is my tenth year coming to CES," he said. "And I barely made it to the exhibit floor this year."

That caught my attention. "But isn't one of the biggest draws of the conference to see the newest technology?"

He sat in the chair next to me. "I used to spend all day at the show making sure I saw every booth, on a mission to see every new tech invention. I would treat it like a relay race. But over the years, I realized something: I was doing it all wrong. The best part of the conference isn't in the products on display—it's the people displaying them."

It was so simple yet so profound. I closed my laptop, eager to hear more. "What do you mean by that?"

"Well, I run a small electronics company in Japan," he continued. "Every year, I come here to meet with my partners from all over the world. We play golf at our favorite course, enjoy dinner together, and catch up on each other's lives." He paused, taking a sip of his coffee. "Today's meeting was with a partner I met eight years ago at CES. Back then, he was running a tiny startup. Now he's one of our biggest suppliers."

The boarding announcement for his flight to Tokyo interrupted our conversation and, as he gathered his things, he turned to me one last time and said, "Always remember—your relationships are your most valuable asset."

As he walked off, I realized that's where I had been going wrong. *I hadn't focused enough on my relationships.* On the flight back to Hawaii, I vowed to never again make the mistake of seeing business as transactional. If I wanted to succeed in business, I *had* to make it personal.

The Business of Being Personal

I've worked in technology for over 20 years, and there is a pattern I keep seeing most founders miss: We often overvalue innovation and undervalue connection. In our pursuit of the latest and greatest innovations, we often overlook what truly lasts—relationships. It's *not* that innovation doesn't matter, but without personal relationships, you are building a rocket ship with no fuel.

Choosing to put people at the heart of everything I did reshaped my career and led to incredible success. By prioritizing relationships, I built trust with clients, partners, customers, employees, lawyers— even my tax accountant. And that trust became the foundation for every major deal I've made.

Business is about people—their goals, fears, and ambitions. It's the connections we make and the trust we build.

A decade after my epiphany in Vegas, I was reminded of this lesson in the middle of a high-stakes transaction. My company, Adconion

Direct, had just been acquired by Amobee for $235 million. Alongside our acquisition, the tech company Kontera, based in Tel Aviv, was also brought into the fold for $150 million, merging two businesses from vastly different worlds.

Given my global management experience, I was appointed president of the newly combined entity, meaning 100 engineers in Israel now reported to me. I wanted my first meeting with the two cofounders to feel like a new beginning, a moment of shared unity and celebration. So, as the sun was coming up in California and setting in Tel Aviv, we met for the first time, via video.

I introduced myself with my usual upbeat energy. "Hi! I'm Kim. I'm so excited to be working with you guys. I know this transition brings a lot of uncertainty, and I want you to know I'm here to learn about everything that's already made you so successful."

My enthusiasm was met with quiet, guarded expressions. The founders were reserved and formal, offering only dry replies; and there I was, the bubbly California gal who prides herself on being unconventional, probably talking too much to fill the lulls in conversation. I tried to ask questions to spark a real dialogue, but it all fell flat. I knew we were in different time zones, but I didn't anticipate that we'd feel worlds apart. The conversation was stilted. But I didn't give up on forging a real connection. So, I pivoted to a more easygoing approach. I tried (and failed) to crack a joke. I asked about their team, their star employees, and their vision for the future. All I received were terse, one-word answers. It felt like I was playing rock music at a ballet recital.

I understood their skepticism. To them, I represented corporate structure and bureaucracy. They didn't trust that I wasn't going to change what made them unique and successful. And they weren't used to having a boss they had to report to.

I got off that call and felt a knot tighten in my stomach. I felt enormous pressure, knowing I needed to lead this team and hit the revenue projections we had promised. The stakes couldn't have been higher. If we couldn't make this acquisition a success, the $385 million investment would be wasted. How was I going to lead and inspire a 100-person team, let alone two founders who didn't trust me, from over 8,000 miles away? The answer was clear: by building a personal relationship.

Days later, I boarded the 15-hour flight from LA to Tel Aviv. I researched everything about the two founders and the company, reading every article I could find. I wanted to understand their story intimately, know why they started their business, and find common ground.

After landing in Tel Aviv, I encountered its famously thorough security process where the customs agents are known for their personal, often probing questions. It's not just about where you're going but what brings you to Israel, and who you're meeting. It's a reminder that in that part of the world, building trust starts at the airport.

The customs agent gave me the same look I'd seen in that video meeting with the founders. *"Four days?"* he asked, studying my passport. *"That's all you need?"* Something in his doubt energized me.

"No, four days is just the start," I told him. "But you have to start somewhere."

As I walked into the Kontera office later that morning, I wore my biggest smile even though I was exhausted from the trip. I thought our first meeting was going to be in the conference room but they had other plans. "First, let's eat," they said.

They took me to their favorite lunch spot and, over the biggest bowl of hummus and most delicious laffa bread I've ever had, we started to get to know each other on a personal level. The shift in energy was transformative; suddenly, we were on equal footing. It was no longer just a formal, distant conversation but an authentic connection. We had so much more in common than we had thought, and we could relate deeply to the Herculean effort it took to reach this point in each other's journey. I now understood that their company, built from scratch over a decade, was the equivalent of their child, and that they had poured everything into making it successful. They were worried about how their culture and identity would fit into a larger structure. When I told them that I had those same fears when my first company got acquired, and that I'd been in the same position and had the same worries, they relaxed. That common ground—that empathy—made all the difference.

Over the next three days, we laid the foundation for what would grow into an incredible working relationship (and eventually a lifelong friendship). There was no doubt that we all wanted this merger to succeed; we simply needed to assume positive intent and trust each other to make it happen.

———————

Nothing can replace the power of in-person connections—the subtle nuances, body language, and candid, confiding moments. Today, digital communication and remote work have created new challenges to maintaining and fostering meaningful relationships. So many businesses rely on Slack, Asana, and Zoom as primary connection points. While these are great tools for optimizing efficiency, they also stand in the way of deepening connections. The reality of the modern world is that we now have to work a lot harder to step outside the screen—and to be more personal.

Steve Jobs always emphasized the importance of engaging face-to-face whenever possible. "There's a temptation in our networked age to think that ideas can be developed by email and iChat," he said. "That's crazy. Creativity comes from spontaneous meetings, from random discussions."

I worry that while we are gaining technological advancements, we risk losing the human connections that bring meaning to business. And I fear that screens and devices are creating those barriers to true creativity and connection.

How many dinners have you gone to where you've seen people staring at their screens instead of talking to each other? I occasionally catch myself doing it, too—unconsciously reaching for my phone, even in a moment meant for connection. We're all navigating this new world where dating usually starts on an app rather than chance encounters. Job interviews often happen online rather than in an office. And first impressions at work frequently happen over Slack instead of at in-person meetings. I think about all the unexpected conversations with cab drivers over the years—stories of their dreams that would have been missed if I'd been looking down at my phone.

When we close ourselves off from these spontaneous moments, we miss the coincidences and conversations that remind us how much we share and how much we have in common. Technology has given us incredible ways to stay connected, but it also gets in the way of us sharing meaningful connections and moments, at work, at home, and socially. I'm not against embracing technology. I've built my career on championing innovation. I'm just advocating for a balance.

When you remember that business *is* personal, and you approach everything with a relationship-first mindset, you are tapping into the secret sauce of success. I've gone to great lengths to build personal connections, and I can confidently say it pays off tenfold. I'll hop on a flight to New York just for dinner, make a stop in an out-of-the-way city to meet in person, or even play 18 holes of golf (despite being terrible at golf) for the sake of connecting face-to-face. I'll go that extra mile because bringing the personal touch matters. And it doesn't have to be as drastic as flying to Tel Aviv. In fact, the tiniest actions can create the biggest impact.

The Little Things Are Big Things

A common mistake I see people make is underestimating the impact of a small, thoughtful gesture. A handwritten thank-you note for going above and beyond, a sincere compliment on a project someone has worked hard on, or remembering a birthday or anniversary and sending flowers—it's the little things that create the building blocks of trust and loyalty, making people feel seen and valued.

At every company I've led, I made sure to recognize the small wins along the way. I've purposefully made it a leadership practice to tell people on a regular basis how much I appreciate their effort and value their contributions. A simple "great job" or a sincere "thank you" can make a world of difference to someone's day. It might seem inconsequential, but not to the employee who has worked tirelessly on a big project. Compliments are free, and they are a meaningful way to recognize someone for their hard work. And here's the thing: When people notice you are paying attention to the little things, it creates lasting goodwill. Never lose sight of daily opportunities for kindness and thoughtfulness. You'll see and feel the difference it makes to everyone around you.

Empathy Improves Leadership

"You see that couple over there?" my dad said, pointing across the road. I nodded as a man and woman, probably in their late 70s, crossed the street, arm in arm.

I was 10 and we were sitting on a set of steps at Pioneer Place, a shopping mall in downtown Portland, Oregon. We had some time to kill while my mom and my sister wandered the stores, so my dad used it as an opportunity for another round of his favorite pastime, "the people game": picking out passersby and imagining their stories, their thoughts, or what their day might have been like.

"What adventures do you think they've had?" he said. "What do you think they're thinking about right now?"

"Use your imagination. Get creative, Kim."

So I created a story about their hometown, their dreams, their daily struggles. "Good," he said, and he pointed to someone new: a mother juggling three kids, and then a man arguing intensely on his phone. "What's going on with them?"

He played this game everywhere we went. Like most of his "games," it had a deeper purpose: encouraging us to see the world through someone else's eyes. He was quietly cultivating our empathy muscle, one story at a time. When you are focused on other people, it stops you from thinking only about yourself. "The more you try to understand others," he'd say, "the better chance you'll have of truly connecting to them."

The lessons in empathy from my dad never left me. If anything, they shaped the way I saw the world, carrying me through college and into adulthood with an instinctive curiosity about what other people were feeling or experiencing in any given situation. I like to believe that this made me a more compassionate leader—one who truly listens, supports, and values the people I work with. People light up when they feel like someone genuinely wants to understand their perspective. Call it human psychology, call it being respectful—the moment you lean in with real curiosity, something shifts. The walls come down. Trust grows.

As Amobee scaled to over 1,000 employees globally, my bandwidth got increasingly stretched thin, and my capacity for empathy started to suffer.

Building a close-knit team and nurturing culture was easier in the beginning when we had a team of 50 in the San Diego office. But as we expanded across 20 offices and multiple time zones globally, the intimate high-touch leadership style that had become my hallmark grew harder to maintain. As time became more scarce, I found myself becoming more transactional and distant and focused solely on getting things done. It wasn't until a disillusioned employee called me out that I realized I had completely missed her cries for help.

Rachel, one of my best-performing employees, had dropped hints about feeling stressed due to an ongoing conflict with her new manager. If I'm honest, I knew there was unease between them but thought it would resolve itself—mainly because I believed Rachel wouldn't take any nonsense and would handle it herself. She had emailed me a few times, but I thought she just wanted to vent and, with my limited bandwidth, her emails went unanswered. Plus, I was already drained from trying to close another acquisition, so the idea of dealing with "people issues" felt too emotionally exhausting. I shouldn't have felt blindsided when her resignation letter landed on my desk, but I did. I immediately called her to convince her to stay, but Rachel's mind was made up.

"I've been trying to let you know, Kim, but you weren't listening," she said.

She reminded me how many times she had tried to get my attention. At that moment, I knew that I had not been the compassionate leader I aspired to be. I looked at her and said, "I'm so sorry that I missed the signs. I'm sorry I let you down."

I couldn't have been any more disappointed in myself. I had failed to take the time to step back, truly listen, and realize just how untenable things had become. I was so consumed with keeping everything moving that I missed the cracks forming beneath the surface.

Her departure was a wake-up call, and I vowed to never again let business distract me from meeting the needs of the important people around me. A decade earlier, after my Vegas trip, I had promised myself to always put people first—but actions clearly didn't reflect that belief. The experience taught me to proactively check in not only with my teams on a regular basis but with the important people in *all areas* of my life. If I was serious about making people a priority, I needed to be more intentional. I needed to be as good as my word.

I recommitted myself to making a conscious effort to give people my full, undivided attention when speaking with them. More than that, when having one-on-one conversations, I put my phone away so I wasn't distracted. I placed my attention fully on the person facing me, ensuring I actively listened to where they were coming from. It didn't take long for my friends and family to notice the difference, too; they told me I seemed more "present," less scattered, and more engaged. And I felt the difference, as well—I felt more connected to those around me. It's easy to get caught up in the day-to-day, but it's important not to forget that people are your greatest asset.

Human connection is the bedrock of everything we build.

Empathy underpins that connection, and it isn't just a "soft skill"; it's essential for building trust and driving success. Studies show that 76% of people who experience empathy from their leaders report being more engaged at work.[34] Brené Brown says that empathy is a choice. "Because, in order to connect with you, I have to connect with something in myself that knows that feeling," she says.

This is why we find ourselves deeply moved by stories in movies. It's not just entertainment; it's a mirror to our own emotions. We cheer when Rocky fights his way to victory, because we see the grit it takes to get up after getting knocked down. We understand Erin Brockovich's fury, because we've felt that same frustration when facing injustice. And in *Jerry Maguire*, we empathize with the risk and hope in following dreams.

Shared experiences fortify empathy. If you haven't gone through a crushing heartbreak, you can't really know what someone is going through. Same with the devastation of being laid off. Or the grief of losing a loved one. Or the terror of going to the brink of bankruptcy. We have to experience these things ourselves, and what we experience

has the ability to bring us closer together. All we need to do is be willing to step into someone else's shoes. If we can do more of that, we
will be amazed at the positive difference it makes to our relationships.

Relationships Are Built on Trust

Empathy builds trust, and trust is the foundation of relationships.
Without it, relationships can't grow, let alone prosper. It was the reason I flew to Tel Aviv to meet the co-founders of Kontera. If they
didn't get to sit across from me, recognize my positive intentions, and
understand my values, the acquisition probably wouldn't have gone
smoothly. Trust is not implicit; it has to be earned.

I've heard many co-founders compare launching a startup to
entering a marriage. In many ways, that's exactly what it is—for richer
or poorer, for better or worse. The success of the union hinges on trust.
This also applies to partnerships, collaborations, mentorships, friendships, and any dynamic that involves working together.

Think of the people you trust 100% in your life. I'll bet they've
earned that trust by demonstrating qualities such as integrity, consistency, loyalty, and empathy. When they say they will do something,
they do it. When they make a promise, they keep their word. When
they say they will be there for you, they show up.

Growing up, my grandpa shared a simple yet impactful philosophy that he said was key to building trust: "Do what you say you will
do (DWYSYWD)." It's a principle to live by. If you don't establish
trust, nothing that follows will work. And if you want to experience
success, you will need a rock-solid network of people to support you.
Without it—at home, at the office, in our social circle—it is impossible to be successful.

I wouldn't be where I am today without the employees, friends,
family, clients, partners, and mentors who helped me along the way as

backers, collaborators, sounding boards, and champions. Every deal I've made started as a relationship that was built on trust and developed over time.

Without teamwork, it would be 10 times harder to achieve anything. The greatest sports teams only taste triumph because of how in sync the players are as a unit. When a winning team's performance declines, you hear fans speculate about whether the coach still has what it takes to deliver results. Because when the camaraderie and spirit breaks, everything breaks. It's the same in business. If you foster a culture built on strong relationships and strong connections, your employees will show up differently. Engaged people show up not only to perform but to make a difference. That kind of energy fuels productivity and loyalty.

It's been my experience that making sure employees and teammates understand your motivations and what truly matters to you helps to forge trust. And the reverse is just as important. Your team will believe in you when you take the time to actively listen and make them feel seen, heard, and understood. Trust doesn't happen by accident. It's earned in the moments when motivations align and mutual respect takes center stage.

One of the best leaders I've ever worked with had an uncanny ability to establish trust and respect almost *instantly*—it was his superpower. On his first day as chief operating officer at Amobee, he called an all-team meeting and didn't begin with the usual corporate spiel. He didn't set the tone with his vision for the company or why the role was important to him. Instead, he led with something unexpected: *himself*. He shared stories about his transient childhood—constantly moving from place to place, his love for boating, his obsession with French bulldogs, his family, and his passion for single-malt bourbon. That first impression he made wasn't just relatable—it was disarming.

I admired how willing he was to be open and vulnerable, while, at the same time, conveying authority and capability. In less than an hour, he created an environment of trust because he had demonstrated openness, transparency, and respect. By dropping the corporate mask and showing us who he was, he invited everyone to bring their most authentic selves to work. I encourage others to adopt the mindset in all walks of life: that showing the people around you *who you are* is just as important as why you are there.

The Recipe for Success

I'm sure you've heard people say "Never do business with friends." But when longtime friends and co-workers Sarah Lee and Christine Chang decided to launch a skincare company together, they didn't just ignore this warning—they built a beauty empire by doing the exact opposite.

The two founders met while working at L'Oréal in Korea, and both relocated to the company's New York office years later. They'd often meet up after work and talk about how incredible it would be to make Korean-inspired beauty products available worldwide.

In 2014, with a combined $50,000 in savings, they took the leap from their corporate desks to become entrepreneurs. They didn't just break the cardinal rule of business—never work with friends— they shattered it. "Everyone warned us about mixing friendship and business," Sarah told me. "They were right, but *not* in the way they thought. We didn't want to separate them. Everything we've achieved stems from our foundational friendship."

Instead of following the corporate playbook, Sarah and Christine had a bold strategy: They would build their beauty brand the same way they built their friendship. By making everything personal. *Everything.*

Think about it: When was the last time a CEO personally responded to your Instagram comment? Or sent you a handwritten thank-you note? Or wished you a happy birthday? That's exactly what Sarah and Christine did.

The more personal they got, the bigger they grew. While other companies were experimenting with automated customer service systems, Glow Recipe was handwriting notes and responding personally to social media comments within hours. "Industry veterans warned us it wouldn't scale," Sarah told me. "But what they missed was that authenticity itself is scalable. You just have to be willing to invest in it."

The results? A community that has grown to 4 million loyal followers. And when I say "loyal," I mean *loyal*. How many founders can say their customers have invited them to their weddings? (Yes, that actually happens at Glow Recipe.)

Here's what I find so revolutionary: While most companies start Monday mornings reviewing revenue projections, the global team at Glow Recipe begins with customer success stories. Not sales targets. Not quarterly forecasts. No, they start with human stories. "Because if you forget the human behind those stories, none of the numbers matter," said Sarah.

This priority shift reminds every team member that behind each sale is a real person with a story. That's the secret to their recipe—the people. When you start with people, the profits follow. Glow Recipe's $300 million in annual revenue isn't just a number—it's proof that in an age of automation, the personal touch might be the most effective business strategy of all. So the next time someone tells you not to make business personal, remember Glow Recipe. Sometimes, the best way to succeed isn't to follow the rules—it's to rewrite them entirely.

Mastering Relationship Building: The I-CARE Framework

Developing lasting business relationships is a strategy in itself, and it's one that requires time, care, and attention. For that reason, I've created the I-CARE (investment, curiosity, active listening, relatability, empathy) framework. It's not just a tool to keep me on track; it's a guide for anyone who wants to build real, lasting connections with the people who matter most—clients, employees, mentors, partners, even friends. Because at the end of the day, relationships aren't just part of the job—they *are* the job.

I–Investment

I've always said that I don't invest in companies. I invest in people. But I've learned that true connections don't develop overnight, and building relationships takes effort. When establishing new relationships, I make it a priority to invest time up front to build a strong foundation. A helpful practice is to identify five of your most critical working relationships and prioritize regular check-ins. Whether it's a quick catch-up call, a meeting for a casual coffee or happy hour, or sending a voice note to check In, these moments add up. Investing your time, energy, and attention helps to foster trust and reinforce your commitment to growing the relationship.

C–Curiosity

When I meet new people, I make it a point to come with a curious mind. Being curious means asking questions from a genuine place of interest. I spend the majority of the conversation trying to understand their world—their goals, passions, hobbies, and what makes them tick.

This fosters a solid foundation for a relationship because it shows that I value their opinions and experiences. Curiosity isn't just about gathering facts; it's about understanding people. We all remember those conversations where someone has shown a genuine interest in who we are and what we have to say; it leaves a positive, lasting impression.

A—Active Listening

The art of listening is becoming a forgotten art, but it's an essential one to practice if you are going to build genuine relationships. As my mom often said, "You have two ears and one mouth—use them in that order." While curiosity opens the doors, it's the attentiveness that follows that truly matters. As Simon Sinek puts it: "Listening is not the act of hearing the words spoken; it's the art of understanding the meaning behind those words." As he says, the important thing is that the other person feels heard. That requires you to be fully present so you can pay attention to their words, tone, and body language. I take notes (logging them in my phone) for personal details like birthdays, family members, favorite sports teams, and hobbies, so I can recall them the next time we connect. When someone realizes you've remembered something meaningful to them, they're far more likely to remember you.

R—Relatability

Relating to people on a personal level is a key to building enduring relationships. When we discover shared experiences or interests with someone, it becomes easier to relate. I've found that the more I ask about topics *beyond work*, the better able I am to find opportunities to connect with others. Whether it's discovering a shared favorite musician, bonding over parenting challenges, or swapping recommendations for books or restaurants, these seemingly small connections can create a foundation of trust that extends beyond the professional realm. Personal connections humanize professional interactions and make them more memorable. Demonstrating genuine interest in someone's experiences and passions can differentiate you from competitors and open doors to new opportunities.

E–Empathy

Empathy isn't just a feel-good concept; it's a powerful tool for connection. By putting yourself in someone else's shoes, you can better understand their perspective. Whatever situation arises or whatever opinion is expressed, always try to see it from the other person's point of view. This immediately softens any interaction, grounding it in kindness and understanding. When you approach relationships with empathy, you demonstrate that you value the other person's thoughts, feelings, and experiences; in turn, this paves the way for open and honest communication. And that is how empathy is best demonstrated—by how you communicate. Being sensitive to someone else's experience, emotions, or thoughts, and having the ability to express that understanding, is a powerful skill that strengthens bonds and builds loyalty. Empathy transforms interactions from transactional to meaningful.

Your True Business Advantage

When you make business personal, you create a powerful competitive advantage. The story of Glow Recipe is a testament to how much of an asset it can be if you look at everything through the lens of relationships. I love the way social marketing strategist Ted Rubin frames it. He champions the idea that businesses should think beyond traditional ROI (return on investment) and instead embrace a new model—ROR (return on relationship).

Where ROI measures direct financial returns from products or campaigns, the value in ROR "accrues over time through connection, trust, loyalty, recommendations, and sharing." It is, says Rubin, "the difference between capturing immediate financial gains and fostering long-term benefits that aren't solely focused on the revenue sheet."[35] His point is clear: If you get the relationships right, you have more satisfied customers, more positive word of mouth, and a brand remembered for how it treats people.

Staying focused on the numbers is essential, but you can do this while also building long-term relationships. As Ted says, you can use ROI to focus on measurable financial outcomes, but the return on relationships—by fostering trust, loyalty, and engagement—can have its own measurable value.

Think back to the last time you had a great experience as a customer, consumer, or fan, and remember how it made you *feel*. Maybe you were at a restaurant, and the server was so attentive and personable that you felt genuinely valued. Or perhaps a brand went beyond expectations by including a personalized note or a free gift in a package, leaving a lasting impression. Often, we remember a business not just for its product but for the personal touches—a memorable interaction, gesture, or thoughtful detail that made us feel seen. That's ROR (return on relationship) in action.

I'm often asked, "What's your secret? How did you become so successful?"

Most people think I'm going to say it was an early bet on digital advertising or a savvy investment. But the truth is: I didn't make millions because I had the best business plan or the most cutting-edge technology. It's because I chose to make business personal. With a grandmother who believed in me enough to write that first $10,000 check. With my employees who stayed for the late nights and believed in my vision to build something from nothing. With my clients who trusted me with their business strategies. With my partners who stood beside me through both triumphs and setbacks. And with my high school and college friends who have stood by my side with unconditional support. My success has been dependent on the relationships I forged and what I gave back to those relationships. To quote Zig Ziglar, "You can have everything in life you want if you'll just help enough other people get what they want."

Every deal I've closed, every company I've built, every milestone I've reached, every person I have mentored—they all trace back to moments of genuine connection. To conversations over hummus in Tel Aviv. To handwritten thank-you notes. To remembering birthdays and celebrating small wins. To showing up when it matters most. My dad was right all those years ago: When you truly see people—when you try to understand their stories and struggles and dreams—that's when business transcends transactions and becomes transformation.

Remember this: Strong relationships are the key to lasting success. The numbers matter, but people matter more. Strategies count, but the relationships count more. They're what makes it all worthwhile. They're what makes it all meaningful. They're what makes it personal.

LESSON IN THE MISTAKE

Data can tell you what's profitable, but relationships determine what's possible.

CHAPTER SUMMARY

Self-reflection: How well do you prioritize personal relationships in business and life in general? How do you bring the human touch to everything you do? How comfortable are you showing empathy and vulnerability?

Key Takeaways:

▶ **Business IS Personal:** Don't buy the myth that business isn't personal. It always is. Nothing replaces the power of in-person connection, so bring realness and authenticity to every deal, project, and partnership.

▶ **Relationships Drive Success:** Success is built on genuine human connections. Step into the shoes of someone else to cultivate empathy. Keep your word, show up, and be consistent to earn trust. Lead with integrity and honesty, and watch your relationships thrive.

▶ **Focus on the Little Things:** The tiniest things can have the biggest impact. Small, simple gestures—a thank-you note, a compliment, remembering a birthday—all add up as little building blocks of loyalty. Make sure you are remembered for your thoughtfulness.

▶ **Face-to-Face Meetings Matter:** Nothing can replace the power of in-person connections—they foster trust and understanding in ways that email, Zoom, or calls can't replicate. Embracing technology shouldn't mean abandoning the human touch.

▶ **Get Personal:** Share your personal story, hobbies, and interests in conversations to create genuine connections, strengthen relationships, and build trust quickly.

▶ **Implement the I-CARE Framework:** If you truly care about developing your relationships, adopt the I-CARE framework. Invest time. Show curiosity. Actively listen. Relate on a personal level. Empathize. People will feel the difference.

Millionaire Mindset: I believe that true success is built on meaningful connections and showing genuine care for others. I strive to leave a legacy that leads with kindness, loyalty, and generosity.

Make Mistakes Your Superpower

You already know the undeniable truth: Mistakes are not the enemy. They are the raw materials of success, the stepping stones to something greater.

While the mistakes in this book shaped my journey to success, this story isn't just about me. It's about you! It's about the mistakes you will make and how they will shape your future. Every mistake has the power to teach you, sharpen your skills, and lead you to the breakthroughs that create not just a fulfilling life but real wealth.

When you find yourself making the same mistakes, I hope you will pull wisdom from my experience and know you will get through it, too. You don't need a perfect business plan, a flawless track record, or decades of experience to make millions. You need the willingness to learn, the courage to act, and the resilience to keep going when others would quit.

Mistakes aren't optional; they're inevitable. You'll miscalculate. You'll hesitate when you should act—or act when you should pause. You'll pick the wrong people, hold on to things for too long, and walk away from opportunities too soon. But the good news is this: Your mistakes don't define you. How you *respond* to them does.

The mistakes in this book gave me so much more than financial success. My mistakes gave me courage. They gave me humility. They gave me clarity. They made me stronger, smarter, and more prepared for whatever came next.

Every mistake I made taught me something invaluable.

Waiting to feel 100% ready taught me that perfection is the enemy of progress. Trying to do everything alone showed me the power of surrounding myself with supportive people. Being paralyzed by fear revealed that courage isn't the absence of fear—it's taking action despite it.

The painful lesson of picking the wrong people taught me to trust my gut. Staying too long taught me when to let go. Failing to pivot taught me the power of adaptability. And believing I was underqualified? That taught me that our biggest limitations are often self-imposed. Each mistake was a lesson wrapped in an experience, waiting to be unwrapped by someone brave enough to learn from it.

And guess what? I am not done making mistakes. This book is not the end of my mistake journey—it's just another chapter. I will keep making mistakes. Because success isn't about getting everything right. It's about continuing to move forward even when things go wrong.

As you close this book and step back into your world, I want you to make yourself a promise. Promise you'll start before you're ready. Promise you'll stop seeing mistakes as failures and start seeing them as feedback. Promise you'll embrace the discomfort of growth instead of the comfort of staying the same. Promise me you will find a mentor. Promise that when things go wrong—and they will—you'll ask yourself: "What will I make from this mistake?" This simple question invites multiple possibilities: growth, reinvention, pivots, opportunities. It isn't just about *learning* from mistakes, it's about *leveraging* them.

The next chapter of your life won't be written by avoiding mistakes—it will be written by embracing them. I'm not saying it's easy, but I'm telling you that I'm 100% sure you will grow stronger with every mistake you make.

This is your moment. Your time to take risks. Your opportunity to make magnificent mistakes. Your chance to turn setbacks into comebacks.

Don't wait for perfection—it never arrives.

Don't wait for permission—it's already yours.

Don't wait for certainty—the only certainty is there is none.

So here's my challenge to you: Make bold mistakes. Be audacious. Take brave actions. The power of transformation lies in your hands. Your mistakes will forge you into someone stronger, wiser, and more capable than you ever imagined possible. I know you will one day look back and celebrate how far you've come . . . as well as all the mistakes you made along the way. Just like I have.

Remember: Mistakes aren't the end—they're the beginning!

Kim

Acknowledgments

Bringing *Mistakes That Made Me a Millionaire* to life has been an unforgettable journey filled with lessons, laughter, and, of course, plenty of mistakes along the way. But one thing I got absolutely right? The all-star team that helped turn this vision into reality.

I wasn't 100% ready to start writing in 2023, but I had 70% of the ideas in my head—and that was enough. From there, I made sure to pick the right people who would guide me every step of the way, and I'm deeply grateful to everyone involved.

To my husband, John, my lifelong partner and greatest champion—thank you for your unwavering love and encouragement. You remain the best decision I ever made. And to our four incredible children—Elle and John, and Bill and Jack—your love, curiosity, and laughter inspire me every single day.

To my parents, whose love and wisdom shaped me long before my mistakes ever did—thank you for showing me what resilience and hard work look like. To my twin sister, Tracy, my sounding board and the person who always finds the right words; and my brother, Mark, for always being in my corner, cheering me on.

A heartfelt thank-you to Matt Holt, who saw the potential in this book from the very beginning, along with your stellar team at

BenBella Books: Katie Dickman, Jessika Rieck, Morgan Carr, Ariel Jewett, Rachel Phares, and Brigid Pearson.

To my incredible writing partners, Liv Auerbach and Steve Dennis—your talents are on every page, and I wouldn't have made it to the finish line (or stayed sane) without you. Also, special mention to my mom, whose notes on every chapter were invaluable. And to Doug Wagner for your expert precision and polish.

To Jessie Gardner, for your creative genius in shaping the design, marketing, and overall feel of this book. Your ideas and energy made all the difference.

To Chris Burch, for always answering the call when I needed inspiration. Your wisdom in business and life is something I cherish deeply.

To Marc Randolph, for writing the foreword and for always pushing me to raise my game—on and off set. I'm grateful for your friendship and guidance.

To Sarajane, Tricia, Cari, and Amanda—your friendships, stories, and endless support remind me every day how lucky I am.

To Stephen Power, Kevin Anderson, and Lee Moreau, thank you for championing this book, for your thorough editorial guidance, and for keeping me on track.

To the many relatives, friends, partners, investors, and mentors who have been part of my journey—you may not all be named here, but you know who you are. Your support, encouragement, and wisdom have meant the world to me.

And finally, to you—the reader. You are the reason I wrote this book. Whether you found me through social media, a conference, a business event, or through a mutual network, I'm honored that you've taken the time to sit with these pages. My hope is that this book helps you see that mistakes aren't the end of the road—they're part of your path to success.

Notes

1. Amanda Ruggeri, "The dangerous downsides of perfectionism," BBC, February 20, 2018, https://www.bbc.com/future/article/20180219-toxic-perfectionism-is-on-the-rise.
2. Seth J. Gillihan, "How Often Do Your Worries Actually Come True?," *Psychology Today*, July 19, 2019, https://www.psychologytoday.com/us/blog/think-act-be/201907/how-often-do-your-worries-actually-come-true.
3. "Why do we have a harder time choosing when we have more options?," The Decision Lab, accessed May 28, 2024, https://thedecisionlab.com/biases/choice-overload-bias.
4. Grant A. Pignatiello, et al., "Decision fatigue: A conceptual analysis," *Journal of Health Psychology*, Volume 25, Issue 1 (March 23, 2018), https://pubmed.ncbi.nlm.nih.gov/29569950/.
5. "Brainwork: The Power of Neuroplasticity," Cleveland Clinic, December 13, 2023, https://health.clevelandclinic.org/neuroplasticity.
6. Richa Kalra, "Children may care about their reputations earlier than thought: Study," ABC News, August 27, 2018, https://abcnews.go.com/Health/children-care-reputations-earlier-thought-study/story?id=57403548.
7. "Asking for help is hard, but people want to help more than we realize," *Stanford Report*, September 8, 2022, https://news.stanford.edu/stories/2022/09/asking-help-hard-people-want-help-realize.

8. Luis E. Romero, "The Power of Vulnerability in Leadership," *Forbes*, March 8, 2023, https://www.forbes.com/sites/luisromero /2023/03/08/the-power-of-vulnerability-in-leadership-experts-say -authenticity-and-honesty-can-move-people-and-achieve-results/.

9. "Steve Jobs on Failure" *(Calling Bill Hewlett)*, Silicon Valley Historical Association, YouTube, posted October 31, 2011, https://www .youtube.com/watch?v=zkTf0LmDqKI.

10. Kate Murphy, "Outsmarting Our Primitive Responses to Fear," *New York Times*, October 26, 2017, https://www.nytimes.com/2017 /10/26/well/live/fear-anxiety-therapy.html.

11. Murphy, "Outsmarting Our Primitive Responses to Fear," *New York Times*.

12. "Man in the Arena," Theodore Roosevelt, April 23, 1910, Theodore Roosevelt Center, https://www.theodorerooseveltcenter.org/Learn -About-TR/TR-Encyclopedia/Culture-and-Society/Man-in-the -Arena.aspx.

13. Laura Huang, "When It's OK to Trust Your Gut on a Big Decision," *Harvard Business Review*, October 22, 2019, https://hbr.org /2019/10/when-its-ok-to-trust-your-gut-on-a-big-decision.

14. "Steve Jobs by Walter Isaacson," Arun Kant, Soulveda, April 19, 2018, https://www.soulveda.com/books/steve-jobs-by-walter-isaacson/.

15. Esther Perel, "How Can I End a Friendship?" Instagram video, April 10, 2024, @estherperelofficial.

16. Thomas C. Corley, "I Studied 177 Self-made Millionaires for 5 Years, and I Learned That Rich People Choose Their Friends Differently Than the Rest of Us," Thrive Global, January 31, 2020, https:// community.thriveglobal.com/studied-self-made-millionaires -learned-rich-people-choose-their-friends-differently-wisdom -wealth/.

17. Stephanie Vozza, "7 Habits of Self-Made Millionaires," *Fast Company*, November 16, 2015, https://www.fastcompany.com/3052770 /7-habits-of-self-made-millionaires.

18. "Mentorship statistics you and your business need to know," Upnotch, April 4, 2024, https://www.upnotch.com/post/mentorship-statistics -you-and-your-business-need-to-know.

19. Jackie MacMullan, "The astonishing mentors who shaped Kobe Bryant," ESPN, April 5, 2020, https://www.espn.com/nba/story /_/id/15193525/jordan-russell-kareem-even-king-pop-astonishing -mentors-shaped-kobe-bryant.

20. "Groups Perform Better Than the Best Individuals at Solving Complex Problems," American Psychological Association, 2006, https:// www.apa.org/news/press/releases/2006/04/group.

21. Northwestern Mutual, "U.S. Adults Prefer Playing It Safe Rather Than Taking Risks With Their Money, Careers and Social Lives," PR Newswire, December 11, 2019, https://www.prnewswire.com /news-releases/us-adults-prefer-playing-it-safe-rather-than-taking -risks-with-their-money-careers-and-social-lives-300972273 .html.

22. Greg Iacurci, "Typical job switcher got a pay raise of nearly 10 percent, study finds," CNBC, August 2, 2022, https://www.cnbc .com/2022/08/02/typical-job-switcher-got-a-pay-raise-of-nearly -10percent-study-finds.html.

23. Rakesh Kochhar, Kim Parker, and Ruth Igielnik, "Majority of U.S. Workers Changing Jobs Are Seeing Real Wage Gains," Pew Research Center, July 28, 2022, https://www.pewresearch.org /social-trends/2022/07/28/majority-of-u-s-workers-changing-jobs -are-seeing-real-wage-gains/.

24. Charlotte Nickerson, "The Yerkes-Dodson Law of Arousal and Performance," Simply Psychology, November 9, 2023, https://www .simplypsychology.org/what-is-the-yerkes-dodson-law.html.

25. Traci Purdum (compiled by), "Study: Nearly Half of New Hires Fail," *IndustryWeek*, October 4, 2005, https://www.industryweek .com/the-economy/public-policy/article/21949369/study-nearly -half-of-new-hires-fail.

26. Eva de Mol, "What Makes a Successful Startup Team," *Harvard Business Review*, March 21, 2019, https://hbr.org/2019/03/what -makes-a-successful-startup-team.

27. Owen Hughes, "It's Not Just a Talent Shortage—Employers Admit They're Hiring the Wrong People," ZDNet, April 29, 2022, https:// www.zdnet.com/article/its-not-just-a-talent-shortage-employers -admit-theyre-hiring-the-wrong-people/.

28. Marwa Azab, PhD, "The History of Imposter Syndrome," *Psychology Today*, August 22, 2023, https://www.psychologytoday .com/us/blog/neuroscience-in-everyday-life/202308/the-history-of -imposter-syndrome.

29. "Visualization: The Power of the Movie Theater in Your Mind," Ball Is Psych, January 24, 2019, https://www.ballispsych.com/post /visualization-the-power-of-the-movie-theater-in-your-mind.

30. David Coreen, "The Science Behind Goal Achievement," Davron, January 19, 2024, https://www.davron.net/the-science-behind-goal -achievement/.

31. Jeff Haden, "46 Years Ago, This Forgotten Apple Co-Founder Left an Estimated $75 Billion on the Table," *Inc.*, April 4, 2022, https:// www.inc.com/jeff-haden/46-years-ago-this-forgotten-apple-co -founder-left-an-estimated-75-billion-on-table.html.

32. Stephen King, "Carrie: The Bestseller I Threw in the Bin," *The Guardian*, September 17, 2000, https://www.theguardian.com /books/2000/sep/17/stephenking.fiction.

33. Skin cancer incident rates, published by the American Academy of Dermatology (2024), https://www.aad.org/media/stats-skin-cancer.

34. "Why Having Empathy as a Leader Is Important," American Society of Administrative Professionals, July 5, 2022, https:// www.asaporg.com/leadership/why-having-empathy-as-a-leader-is -important.

35. Ted Rubin, "Return on Relationships Basics," Ted Rubin Straight Talk, August 12, 2023, https://tedrubin.com/return-on-relationship -basics/.

About the Author

Kim Perell is 9X founder, 2X bestselling author, investor in 100+ companies, acclaimed speaker, and a proud mom of four. She started her first company from her kitchen table at 23 years old, became a multimillionaire by the time she was 30, and sold her last company for $235 million.

Kim has dedicated her life to empowering the next generation of business leaders. She shines as a dynamic TV and media personality on *Entrepreneur* magazine's hit show *Elevator Pitch*. Kim regularly appears in media, including *Good Morning America*, the *Today* show, *The Drew Barrymore Show*, CNBC, Fox, MSNBC, *CNNMoney*, *The New York Times*, *Forbes*, *Inc.*, and *The Huffington Post*.

In her latest book, *Mistakes That Made Me a Millionaire*, Kim Perell shares the raw, unfiltered truth about the journey to success—proving that every mistake holds the potential for million-dollar lessons.

Kim is an avid traveler and adventure seeker and lives with her husband in Miami, Florida, with their two sets of twins and 200-pound English mastiff, Bella.

Learn more at KimPerell.com

CONNECT WITH KIM

Let's stay in touch!

1: Join My Weekly Newsletter

Join the next generation of aspiring millionaires and receive exclusive insights, new content, and success hacks delivered to your inbox every week.

Sign up for free at KimPerell.com/Newsletter

2: Unlock Your Millionaire Tool Kit

I've created a collection of free and valuable resources to set yourself up for success.

Access your toolkit at KimPerell.com/Resources

3: Connect on Social

Let's stay in touch. Send me a DM on your favorite social medial platform @KimPerell.